ail

DUMMIES®

by Royal Mail

JOHN WILEY & SONS, LTD

Direct Mail For Dummies®

Published by
John Wiley & Sons, Ltd
The Atrium
Southern Gate
Chichester
West Sussex
PO19 8SQ
England

E-mail (for orders and customer service enquires): cs-books@wiley.co.uk

Visit our Home Page on www.wiley.com

Published by John Wiley & Sons, Ltd, Chichester, West Sussex

For general information on our other products and services, please contact our Customer Care Department within the U.S. at 800-762-2974, outside the U.S. at 317-572-3993, or fax 317-572-4002.

For technical support, please visit www.wiley.com/techsupport.

Wiley also publishes its books in a variety of electronic formats. Some content that appears in print may not be available in electronic books.

ISBN-13: 978-0-470-05906-7

ISBN-10: 0-470-05906-0

Printed and bound in Great Britain by TJ International, Ltd, Padstow, Cornwall

10 9 8 7 6 5 4 3 2 1

WILEY

Publisher's Acknowledgments

We're proud of this book; please send us your comments through our Dummies online registration form located at www.dummies.com/register/.

Some of the people who helped bring this book to market include the following:

Acquisitions, Editorial, and Media Development

Executive Project Editor: Martin Tribe

Development Editor: Daniel Mersey

Custom Publishing Representative: Scott Smith

Executive Editor: Jason Dunne

Cartoons: Ed McLachlan

Composition

Project Coordinator: Kristie Rees

Layout and Graphics: Lauren Goddard, Denny Hager, Stephanie D. Jumper, Barbara Moore, Heather Ryan

Proofreaders: David Faust, Dwight Ramsey, Brian H. Walls

Publishing and Editorial for Consumer Dummies

Diane Graves Steele, Vice President and Publisher, Consumer Dummies

Joyce Pepple, Acquisitions Director, Consumer Dummies

Kristin A. Cocks, Product Development Director, Consumer Dummies

Michael Spring, Vice President and Publisher, Travel

Kelly Regan, Editorial Director, Travel

Publishing for Technology Dummies

Andy Cummings, Vice President and Publisher, Dummies Technology/General User

Composition Services

Gerry Fahey, Vice President of Production Services

Debbie Stailey, Director of Composition Services

Table of Contents

Introduction

If you want to talk to existing or potential new customers on a one-to-one basis, direct mail is the smart choice. This book covers planning, executing, and managing a successful campaign, highlighting common blunders to steer clear of and must-know information to absorb. We tell you exactly why direct mail is so successful and show you how to use it to benefit your company in terms of both relationships with your customers and the all important bottom line. There's some poor direct mail about – and this book is intended to make sure it isn't yours!

About This Book

We've developed this book to provide the practical help and techniques you need to make mailshots work for you and your business. We're working on the assumption that you have little or no experience of direct mail to date, but aim to give you all the practical information you need to make direct mail work for you. The emphasis is on 'practical' though, so roll up your sleeves and get stuck in!

Conventions Used in This Book

To help you navigate through this book, we've used a few conventions to keep things simple:

- *Italic* is used to emphasise important words and highlight new terms that you may not have come across before.
- **Boldface** is used to point out key points in numbered steps and bulleted lists.
- `Monofont` is used for Web addresses, which direct you to further sources of information.

Also, watch out for the shaded grey boxes scattered through the book. These are known as sidebars. The information in these sidebars is deemed interesting but not essential. So you can choose to read a sidebar if the topic appeals to you, but if you skip it, you won't miss out on anything you need to know.

Foolish Assumptions

We had to make a few assumptions about you to make sure you get the most out of this book:

- You understand the importance of promoting your business to existing customers and potential new customers (we refer to these as *prospects*).
- You are interested in direct mail as a way of growing your business.
- You have little or no experience of direct mail.

How This Book Is Organised

Direct Mail For Dummies is divided into five parts, each with its own chapters and sub-sections making information easy to find and, thanks to the bite-sized chunks, easy to digest.

Part I: Understanding How Direct Mail Helps Business

This part shows you why direct mail is such a successful part of any marketing strategy for both small and large businesses. These chapters are especially useful if you're new to direct mail, telling you exactly what it can be used for and who should be using it, allowing you to decide if direct mail's right for your business.

Part II: Planning Effective Mailshots

This part is a guide to planning successful mailshots. In it, you'll find the essential advice you need when you're starting out: how to define your objectives, how to estimate costs, how to reach new and existing customers, and how to get them to respond.

Part III: Writing and Designing Successful Mailshots

Here you'll find lots of useful tips to maximise the impact of style and design. Among other things, you'll find out about writing effective letters, designing envelopes, and laying out leaflets.

Part IV: Sorting Out Production and Dispatch

The print and production side of direct mail is covered in this part, along with what to do when the responses come back (make that, *flooding* back). If you're producing your own mailing this part shows you what to look out for, but also gives useful information about using printers, agencies, buying lists, mailing databases, and handling customer responses.

Part V: The Part of Tens

A *For Dummies* favourite, the emphasis here is on easy-to-digest information. We give ten really interesting things you probably didn't know about direct mail, and suggestions for testing your mailshot's effectiveness.

Icons Used in This Book

Throughout the book we've used icons as a quick visual reference to help you better navigate its contents. Look out for the following ones:

This bull's eye indicates a hint or a shortcut to make your direct mailing life easier.

This icon highlights key bits of direct mail information advice that you really need to take on board.

To aid your understanding, with this icon we give examples of how direct mail works in the real world.

If pushed for time, you can skim through the text accompanied by this icon. It highlights technical information that you don't necessarily need to understand, but adds that little bit extra to your direct mail knowledge.

We've used this icon to pick out a few exercises for you to try out before committing your money, or to test your current direct mail campaign's effectiveness.

Where to Go from Here

Direct Mail For Dummies is not a novel, it's a reference guide! Like all *For Dummies* books, it's designed to give you the most helpful information in the most user-friendly way. You can, of course, read it from cover to cover, but you can also dip in and out. Use the Table of Contents to find the topic most relevant to you and your business, then simply turn to the relevant page.

Depending on what stage you're at in your direct mail campaign, you'll want to start by reading different parts of the book. If you're just getting going, and haven't even decided if direct mail is the right thing for you, start with Part I. But if you're a bit further along and need help with, for example, design, flick straight through to Part III (but maybe stop to look at the cartoons on the way!).

Part I

Understanding How Direct Mail Helps Business

'And to deliver the goods, I bought the postage online—a new company called "Rocket Deliveries".'

In this part . . .

Although interested in direct mail (you wouldn't be reading this book otherwise – we hope!), you still might need some convincing that it's the right business strategy for you. This part shows you the ways that direct mail can benefit your business, whether it's a big or small one, by listing the different things it can be used for. If you're new to direct mail, this is the place to start.

Chapter 1

Getting the Lowdown on Direct Mail

In This Chapter

- Finding out what direct mail is
- Looking at why direct mail works
- Considering what causes a campaign to fail
- Figuring out how direct mail differs from direct marketing

Whether you know it or not, you're already familiar with direct mail, if only because you've received plenty of it through your own letter box. You may even have an idea of what works and what doesn't from the point of view of a recipient. But now you have to step into the shoes of the person generating the mailshot (we use this term interchangeably with direct mail throughout the book). In order to take this step, you need to know a little bit about the nature of the beast and what it commonly achieves – or fails to achieve!

But never fear, *Direct Mail For Dummies* guides you through the direct mail minefield, and this chapter gets you off to a flying start – covering the questions most commonly asked about direct mail.

What Exactly Is Direct Mail?

Direct mail uses the postal system to communicate directly to your customers or prospects. It can be sent to large or small volumes of customers, can be unpersonalised (addressing

'The Homeowner' or unaddressed) or personalised, and sometimes simply keeps customers informed or asks for more information.

In a nutshell, direct mail is a promotional strategy that puts your message in the hands of precisely the people you most want to reach.

Why Is Direct Mail So Effective?

Direct mail can be used for anything you'd like to share with any group of customers or prospects in any area of business. Direct mail's purposes are mainly to acquire and retain customers and encourage them to spend more. Direct mail can be very effective at building a positive image for your business, and at its best, is a highly targeted, highly personal, and highly successful form of marketing. Even better, direct mail is also very cost-effective.

TIP

One of the first things people do when they arrive at home or at work is check their post, so direct mail is one of the easiest ways to get your product instant attention.

REMEMBER

Direct mail has an advantage over most other media. Not only is it a fantastic opportunity to engage with all the senses (compare this to television, which engages only the visual and aural senses), but it also creates an emotional reaction in your customers. Think about it: How do you feel when you receive mail? A twinge of hope and longing? Surprise and excitement? Appreciation and familiarity? A good direct mail campaign plays on all these things.

Direct mail allows you to generate a specific response from targeted groups of customers. It is a particularly useful tool in the hands of small businesses by:

- Focussing resources where they're most likely to produce results
- Measuring how successful campaigns have been
- Testing your approach by seeing what gets the best results before developing a full campaign

A direct mail campaign helps you achieve the following objectives:

- Increasing sales to existing customers
- Building customer loyalty
- Re-establishing contact with lapsed customers
- Generating new business

Thinking about what you want to achieve before you set out on your campaign is crucial to its success. Spend as much time as possible drafting key objectives, and use them to refer back to throughout the campaign.

Can Direct Mail Fail?

Of course, no matter how successful a direct mail is there's no absolute guarantee of success. Here are some of the reasons that direct mail can fail:

- **If the message doesn't hit the spot.** It's all about getting to the right people, and there are different ways to make this more effective. Getting personal is proven to help make campaigns more successful, so whatever steps you can pursue to personalise your mailshot, take them!
- **If your message is confusing.** Too much direct mail is too complicated for it's own good. If you throw five tennis balls at someone, they'll drop the lot. If you throw one, they'll catch it. It's the same with messages.
- **If your direct mail campaign isn't supported by other marketing activities.** Direct mail works well on its own, but it works even better if it is supported by other activities – like telephone follow up, or links to your Web site.
- **If you don't try to carve out a niche for yourself.** For example, don't just replicate what's available at the shop on the corner, make sure your offer is different.

But of course, reading *Direct Mail For Dummies* gives you plenty of ideas for making sure that your campaign is as successful as you want it to be.

Isn't Direct Mail the Same As Direct Marketing?

Direct mail is all about communicating directly to the customer, but *direct marketing* is a much broader category, encompassing many ways of selling to your customers.

Direct mail is just one tool to use as part of your direct marketing strategy. Other direct marketing devices include:

- Television and radio ads that request a response from the audience. For example, adverts prompting you to 'Phone this number now . . .'
- Catalogues displaying items available for purchase directly via the telephone or Web
- Insert cards placed in magazines
- Telemarketing calls
- Internet links directing you to 'Click here to find out more'
- E-mails sent directly to your customer's e-mail addresses

REMEMBER

The results of direct mail aren't guaranteed. A poorly planned or targeted campaign is a waste of money. A badly designed mailshot, for example, could simply end up in the bin. Worse still, it may even irritate your recipients, damaging your business' reputation in your customers' eyes.

Chapter 2

Figuring Out If Direct Mail Is Right for You

In This Chapter

- Deciding whether direct mail is your best option
- Using research to find out if it's the best approach

Direct mail is a very versatile tool adaptable to all sorts of situations . . . but it's not a tool that suits everyone. This chapter gives examples of the type of people who can benefit from using direct mail and helps you decide if direct mail's the right strategy for you.

The best way to work out if direct mail really is for you is by using research. So towards the end of this chapter, we touch upon some tips for conducting research, too.

Looking At Who Direct Mail Best Works For

Whoever you are, and whatever your business, being clear about what you're trying to achieve by using direct mail is absolutely essential.

Here are types of companies that find direct mail effective and what they've achieved by using it:

- **Small businesses.** Direct mail is a cost-effective way of building relationships with old and new customers. So long as you have customer addresses or can get them, you can conduct a successful direct mail campaign.
- **Start-ups.** Direct mail is a great way to get your business off the ground if you're just starting up, with relatively small outlay for potentially high returns. You can even test the waters before taking the leap by organising a direct mail campaign before opening your business.
- **Retailers.** Direct mail is well suited to building customer relationships and developing the reputation of your product, brand, or services. It can really make you stand out from the competition by allowing you to personalise your message.
- **Sales.** If you work in sales you can use direct mail to generate leads to follow up. It's also a great way of launching new products or making customers aware of any changes to your company.
- **Events.** If you're business is driven by events – insurance for instance – then direct mail is the obvious choice for a relevant, timely message.
- **Fundraisers.** Fundraising is one of the areas where direct mail is used most effectively. Over the years, charities have conducted highly successful direct mail campaigns that have helped raise huge amounts of money. And many potential donors feel direct mail's much less intrusive than being approached on the street.

TIP

Don't set your objectives too low or too high – make them realistic and achievable, but also worth the investment. Staggering your objectives, perhaps in a series of direct mail campaigns, is an effective and realistic way of achieving your overall goal.

Tables 2-1 and 2-2 show you how effective direct mail is, selling directly to customers, across a range of different markets. Effectiveness is measured according to the number of responses the campaigns received.

Table 2-1 How Direct Mail Performs to Consumers

Sector	*Response Rate %*
Entertainment and leisure	18.5
Household goods and toiletries	18.1
Food and drink	17.3
Automotive industry	13.4
Charity sector	13.0
Pharmaceutical industry	12.8
Gardening and DIY	12.1
Household appliances	11.7
Travel and consumer	11.6
Luxury goods	9.8
Utilities	7.8
Mail order	7.7
Publishing	7.4
Personal loans sector of the financial industry	7.4
Banks and building societies sector of the financial industry	7.2
Insurance sector within the financial industry	7.1
Investment sector of the financial industry	4.5
All direct mail campaigns to consumers 2005	12.1

Source: DMIS Response Rates Survey 2005

Table 2-2 How Direct Mail Performs in Business to Business

Sector	*Response Rate %*
Office supplies	17.2
Travel and entertainment	17.2

(continued)

Table 2-2 *(continued)*

Sector	***Response Rate %***
Industrial equipment	15.8
Business research	15.2
Courses, conferences, and exhibitions	11.6
Marketing services	11.0
Office equipment	10.2
Business services	9.9
Financial services	9.8
Industrial supplies	8.9
Books and magazines	7.9
Office furniture	7.1
Medical services and equipment	6.9
Telecommunications and mobile phones industry	6.0
I.T.	5.2
All direct mail campaigns in business-to-business sector, 2005	10.9

Source: DMIS Response Rates Survey 2005

For more detailed information about working out your objectives and planning in general, read the next section ('Getting Down to Brass Tacks').

Getting Down to Brass Tacks

Before you begin a direct mail campaign, sit down and work out who you want to talk to, and why, and what will make them respond. Make sure you can answer the customer's question, 'What's in it for me?'

Research may seem like an expensive option but direct mail campaigns can fall at the first hurdle if the market intelligence is not right.

If you think of the potential returns, pre-campaign research is well worth the investment. And best of all, you can do it yourself. Here are some great ideas to kick start your research:

- **Contact some of your existing customers to find out what they like best about the product you intend promoting.** Ask them if they'd buy it again, whether they'd recommend it to others, and whether they can think of ways in which the product can be improved.
- **Send out a simple survey rather than conducting research over the phone.** Make it as simple as possible with clear instructions and, where possible, tick boxes. Surveys can achieve the same results as phoning customers, but can be done at your customer's convenience.
- **Find out some personal details about your customers to build up a picture of the type of people you're going to mail.** Ask them whether they're male or female, how old they are, where they live, whether they're employed, about their income, about their education, how they spend their leisure time, and what they've purchased through the mail. Combine this with either of the methods outlined in the previous two bullet points for added convenience.
- **Keep a file with all the direct mail you receive from other businesses and pay attention to your own responses to them.** After all, you're a customer too, and it's always a good idea to keep an eye on what other people are up to. Think about which ones work for you and why. This way you gain an insight into what makes a good mailshot.

Once you've gathered this information and decided that direct mail is definitely an avenue you want to pursue you can move on to the more detailed planning stage. Part II of this book ('Planning Effective Mailshots') helps you get up and running.

Part II
Planning Effective Mailshots

'A great advertising gimmick, George, but who's going to see it up here on top of Everest?'

In this part . . .

This part gives you the practical help, ideas, and techniques you need to make mailshots work most effectively for you and your business. We provide lots of straightforward step-by-step information for you to put into practice immediately. Time to get started!

Chapter 3

Deciding What You Need and What This Costs

In This Chapter

- Defining your objectives
- Calculating the costs
- Analysing your break-even costs and response rates

Before plunging headlong into a direct mail campaign, taking some time to work out what you wish to achieve from it, and how much you can afford to spend on it, pays dividends in the end. And working out what profit you hope to make from your mailshot is worthwhile too!

This chapter leads you through the basics of planning, and as Hannibal from The A-Team once said, 'I love it when a plan comes together!'

Working Out Your Own Direct Mail Objectives

What should your direct mail objectives be? In short, you want more customers and more sales. But how many more? What can you reasonably expect to achieve? Are you going for long-term goals, such as building the reputation of your business, or do you want something more concrete, such as turning customers into repeat customers?

More ideas for your direct mail objectives

What do you wish to achieve? Here's a list of some more suggestions for deciding on the objective of your direct mail campaign:

- Encouraging customers to visit your business or your Web site
- Introducing your business to new customers
- Encouraging referrals from existing customers
- Introducing new products and services
- Reactivating lapsed customers
- Saying thank you
- Following up a recent purchase
- Asking for feedback
- Increasing sales to existing customers
- Offering customers something new

Working out exactly what your objectives are is an important part of the planning process. If you don't know what you want to achieve, it's impossible to assess how well you've done or how you can improve in the future. If you need a hand in working out what a direct mail campaign could do for you, flick back to Chapter 2 for a few pointers.

Here are some examples of typical mailshot objectives:

- Attracting 100 new enquiries in a month
- Making a gross profit of £5,000 per mailing
- Increasing repeat business by 40 per cent over the course of a year
- Securing 500 new customers in six months

If, when you analyse your results, you find your mailshots underperform, either you set your sights too high or some element of your campaign is just not working. If you think your mailshot might outperform your objectives, you need to plan carefully for increased response.

Take a look at the other chapters in this part, dealing with testing and research. Implementing these tips is an effective way of troubleshooting your campaign, enabling you to assess how effective each element really is.

Considering the Cost of Mailshots

You may well have thought of using direct mail in the past but imagined it would be too expensive, so now's the time to take a realistic look at what exactly an effective mailing costs you.

The cost of a mailshot depends on a range of factors, including:

- How many people you want to reach
- How much material you want to send them
- What sort of material you want to send

Like any other business decision, direct mail is all about cost and return. It's only worth undertaking if the income generated is greater than it costs you to design, produce, and deliver.

The difficulty comes, of course, when the return on your investment is harder to quantify. If, for instance, your objective is to build customer loyalty, working out exactly what this is 'worth' and how much money this loyalty represents is pretty tricky.

Doing your sums

If you're a first-timer, you might want to rein in your enthusiasm slightly and start with a mailshot that's small but perfectly formed.

Let's say you go for 1,000 customers, you decide to do the writing and design yourself, use your own mailing list (rather than buying one), and print the leaflets on your own printer. Look at the example in Table 3-1 to see what it would cost you.

Table 3-1 Cost of Creating a Mailshot Yourself

Item	*1,000 mailings*
List rental	nil
Copy and design fees	nil
Artwork and print	nil
Paper	£18
Envelopes	£20
Postage	£320*
Total cost	**£358**
Cost per mailshot	**£358/1,000 = 36p**

**Based on a First class letter (240mm x 165mm x 5mm thick); 32p/item up to 100g. For more information about other products and discounts, visit* `www.royalmail.com`.

Of course, the costs shown in Table 3-1 are not definitive; and fixed costs such as labour, overheads, premises, equipment, and some materials are not included.

Another example is shown in Table 3-2. This time the mailing consists of a personalised letter, a specially prepared leaflet, and an overprinted envelope. This time, you're using some professional help to produce the leaflet and renting a list of names to send your mailshot to. You're aiming for a slightly larger audience so are considering a more ambitious print run – 5,000 – as well.

Table 3-2 Cost of Creating a Mailshot with Professional Services

Item	*1,000 mailings*	*5,000 mailings*
List rental	£100	£500
Letter print	£95	£300
Leaflet print	£95	£300

Item	*1,000 mailings*	*5,000 mailings*
Artwork	£120	£120
Envelopes	£50	£175
Postage	£320*	£1,320**
Enclosing	£100	£300
Total cost	**£750**	**£2,645**
Cost per mailshot	**75p**	**53p**

**Based on a First class letter (240mm x 165mm x 5mm thick); 32p/item up to 100g.*

***Based on a First class letter (240mm x 165mm x 5mm thick); 26.4p/item up to 100g, with Mailshot 1400 discount. For more information about other discounts and products, visit* `www.royalmail.com`.

No matter what your final print run, some costs are at a fixed rate. For example, in Table 3-2, the cost of artwork remains the same for 5,000 mailings as it is for 1,000 mailings, as it's a one-off fee. But for items such as envelopes, printing, and list rental, the prices rise when the number of mailings increases.

Deciding whether direct mail is worth the cost

Once you've done the sums, you'll be able to work out if a direct mail campaign is worthwhile for your objective.

Of course, there's no way of knowing exactly what response you'll get, but this gives you a pretty good idea.

When working out your projected response, bear in mind that existing customers are two times more likely to respond than prospects are:

- To an existing customer: 6 per cent
- To your own prospect list: 3 per cent
- To a rented prospect list: 3 per cent

Calculating break-even

Unless you're happy to send out a mailshot with no eye on the profit or loss you'll make, calculating that your campaign covers its own cost is pretty important.

Break-even analysis works out exactly what you need to make to cover costs, in terms of response rate, profit margin, mailing size, number of sales, and average order value. It's a really useful way to organise your mailshot budget.

Table 3-3 shows an example of a break-even analysis for a mailshot of 1,000 mailings.

Table 3-3 Setting a Break-Even Budget for an Office Supplier

Size of mailshot	***1,000 mailings***
Four per cent response rate	40 replies
25 per cent conversion rate	10 orders
Average order value	£150
Total order value	£1,500
30 per cent profit margin	£450
Resulting break-even budget (total)	£450
Unit cost per mailing	**45p**

Working out your break-even budget involves making some assumptions, such as *conversion rates* (the percentage of people who buy, compared to the percentage of people who respond). So, for example, if 80 people respond and 12 actually buy, your conversion rate is 15 per cent.

In Table 3-3, we assumed that out of the 1,000 people mailed, 40 responded, a quarter of whom bought the product. If each sale is worth £150 at a profit margin of £45 per sale, you'll make £450. If the costs for the mailing exceed £450, you'll fail to break-even. If they come in at under £450 or you get more than 10 orders, congratulations, you're in profit!

Tables 3-4 and 3-5 give another couple of examples using a slightly different working method, starting off by deciding how much you can afford to spend and then working backwards to calculate:

- What profit margin you need to cover costs
- What response rate you need to cover costs

This form of break-even analysis is really useful if you have a fixed budget in mind.

Table 3-4 Checking Your Profit Margin Covers Your Costs

Mailshot budget	£450
Size of mailshot	1,000
Four per cent response rate	40 replies
25 per cent conversion rate	10 orders
Average order value of £150	£1500 in sales
Profit needed to cover costs	£450
Break-even profit margin	**30 per cent**

Envelopes at the ready!

Here are some useful exercises to help you prepare for your mailshot:

- Think about your organisation's current business objectives. Write down three objectives for your mailshots campaign that would help you achieve these.
- Calculate your own cost breakdown for producing a simple mailshot to 500 existing customers.
- Assume a mailing of 1,000, a response rate of 10 per cent, a conversion rate of 20 per cent, and average order value of £250 and a profit margin of 40 per cent, and work out total break-even budget and the unit cost per mailshot.

So, in the example shown in Table 3-4, your profit margin needs to be 30 per cent or higher to cover the costs of your mailshot. Table 3-5 works this the other way to get to a break-even response.

Table 3-5 Setting a Break-Even Response Rate

Mailshot budget	£450
Size of mailshot	1,000 mailings
Profit needed to cover costs	£450
Sales needed at 30 per cent profit	£1500
Average order value of £150	10 orders
25 per cent conversion rate	40 replies
Break-even response rate	**4 per cent**

You control how much you spend on your mailshots, because you control how many people you send your message to. Even if your budget is tight, mailshots are worth sending because they are a great use of resources. You can create your own simple mailshot for little more than the price of a piece of paper, an envelope, and a stamp, so if you wanted to send a message to 100 of your best customers, you could do it at relatively little cost.

Make sure you're geared up for the response to your mailshot by speaking to your suppliers (to ensure that you can get enough stock) and all your staff. Not fulfilling your customer's expectations or even partially fulfilling them can have dire consequences for future sales and your reputation.

Chapter 4

Targeting Your Audience

In This Chapter

- Finding the right customers to approach
- Approaching external suppliers to expand your audience
- Storing customer information safely and legally

If you're planning your first direct mail campaign, existing customers are the best people to send your mailshot to, as they're already interested in your products. But of course, there's a much wider audience out there than just your pre-existing customers, and some mailshots are aimed at bringing in new customers.

This chapter runs through the basics of finding an audience to send mailshots to, expanding this list, and storing information about the people on it.

Making Your Mailing List

Who should you send your mailshots to? The simple answer is anyone you think might be interested in buying your products! These people fall into three categories:

- Existing customers
- Enquirers
- New customers (known as *prospects*)

TIP: Existing customers are a good place to start. They're already warm to your product or service, know your company, have already purchased from you, and are likely to do so again in the future. Existing customers are generally twice as likely to respond to a mailing as new ones (source: Direct Mail Information Service).

Gathering information on enquirers is dealt with in the nest section ('Building up a mailing list from scratch'), and gathering information on new customers is explained in 'Pulling In New Names and Addresses'.

Building a mailing list from scratch

You might think you can't get started on a direct mail campaign because you don't have any customer names or addresses. Are you certain about this? You may not have a ready-made list of customer names and contact information, but most companies have a wealth of untapped information stored in other ways. Good places to check include:

- Accounting systems
- Copies of receipts
- Correspondence files
- Delivery dockets
- Enquiry details or /sales leads
- Sales invoices

REMEMBER

You must comply with certain legal requirements when compiling and collecting data, otherwise you could land yourself in some pretty serious trouble. Have a look at the section 'Keeping Your Records Legal' for more details.

Gathering customer data

If you really don't have the kind of information outlined in 'Building a mailing list from scratch' available, you need to start collecting it. Here are a few ideas on how to go about doing just that:

- **Ask your customers for their details.** Many customers are happy to give you their names and addresses in the process of a phone call to update them about changes to your business.

- **Produce a questionnaire or survey.** These are an excellent way of gathering all sorts of useful information. Figure 4-1 shows a simple template for a customer questionnaire, that you can adapt to your own purposes.

Hargreaves *Butchers*

Customer Survey

At Hargreaves Butchers, we are always aiming to improve our level of service and ensure we offer the kinds of products that you want to buy. Please could you spare a few moments of your time to complete this survey so that we can improve our service to you?

Title ____________ Name ______________________________________
Address ____
____
______________________________ Postcode ______________
Telephone ______________________

Please tick all boxes that apply to you.

Products

Which products do you regularly buy from Hargreaves Butchers?
☐ Beef ☐ Lamb ☐ Pork ☐ Chicken ☐ Cold Meats

Are there any products we don't currently sell, which you would buy from us?
☐ Organic meat ☐ Game ☐ Home-made sausages ☐ Home-made pies
☐ Farm Fresh Eggs ☐ Other (please specify) ______________________

Services

Would you consider using any of the services below if we introduced them?
☐ Telephone ordering ☐ Free doorstep delivery ☐ Late night opening

How often do you shop for your meat products at Hargreaves?
☐ Twice a week ☐ Once a week ☐ Once a fortnight ☐ Once a month

Do you buy from anyone else? ☐ Yes ☐ No

If so, where do you buy them?
☐ Another butcher ☐ Supermarket ☐ Delivery
☐ Other (please specify) ______________________________

What are your primary reasons for buying meat elsewhere?
☐ Better quality ☐ More convenient ☐ Better service ☐ Better range
☐ Longer opening times ☐ Better price ☐ Other (please specify) __________

Please indicate how much you agree/disagree with the following statements.
(5 is strongly agree, 1 is strongly disagree)

I shop at Hargreaves because the quality of the meat is better 1 2 3 4 5
I shop at Hargreaves because I receive better advice 1 2 3 4 5
I like the personal service that comes from dealing with a family business 1 2 3 4 5
Hargreaves is more expensive than its competitors 1 2 3 4 5
I would shop at Hargreaves more often if it opened later 1 2 3 4 5

Figure 4-1: Example of a customer questionnaire.

- **Organise a free prize draw or competition.** There's nothing like the chance of winning a prize to convince customers to part with their details!

  Because of the rules and regulations surrounding data collection (see 'Keeping Your Records Legal', later in this chapter), you need to state clearly on your prize draw or competition what you intend to use the data you collect for. It's also worth knowing that it's illegal to deny a customer entry to your prize draw if they don't want their details entered onto your list. (For more information contact the Direct Marketing Association via `www.dma.org.uk`.)

Pulling In New Names and Addresses

If you want to expand your business beyond the limits of existing customers, you'll need more names and addresses. You can use other approaches to gather the names of potential customers yourself, or you can use an external supplier to source these names for you.

The do-it-yourself approach

The best thing about this way of building up your mailing list is that it's free. The downside is that it's time-consuming and there's no guarantee the people's names you gather will be interested in your business. However, when you're just starting out with a mailshot, this is a good place to begin.

Try building up your own mailing list of potential new customers by using:

- **Street atlases.** If your business is local and you deal mostly with local people, a street atlas provides you with local street names. Simply select an area, check the house numbers on those streets, and post off your mailshot.

  Using a street atlas to drum up new customers lacks the personal touch. Experience shows that mailings without a degree of personalisation generally perform less well than those that have it.

- **Telephone directories.** The phone book is a good source of information as it contains names and telephone numbers, so you can personalise your mailing by addressing it to an individual.

  If you want to mail outside your immediate area, visit your local library – this should hold a complete set of directories for the UK. Of course, there's no supplementary information in them, and regulations restrict the use of information from directories.

- **Business directories.** If you're selling to other businesses rather than members of the public, business directories can be a valuable source of information. They often have more details than simple names and addresses, enabling you to be more selective about the people you include in your mailing. Copies of these directories are often kept in the reference section of public libraries.

- **The electoral register.** Most large public libraries keep a copy of the electoral register. This provides details of people living in a particular area who are registered to vote. You'll be able to gather more information from this source than a telephone directory – for example, how long someone has lived at their current address. Once again, beware of legal restrictions on the use of this information.

- **Online sources.** The Internet is a great way of accessing directories – Web sites such as Yell.com can be very useful, and might save your legs a trip to the library to look at the directories stored there.

- **Other people's lists.** Why not approach a non-competing business in your area and ask if they'd like to swap their list for yours? For example, a sportswear shop could swap its list with a local health and fitness centre. Each one's customers are likely to be interested in the other's products and services. Could you forge a mutually beneficial relationship with someone in your area?

  Check the current regulation relating to list swapping before heading off down this route. For more information contact the Direct Marketing Association via their Web site: `www.dma.org.uk`.

Using an external list supplier

Of course, if you'd rather not do-it-yourself, companies that specialise in developing, compiling, and supplying lists can help you . . . at a cost.

You'll probably deal with a list broker who sources a list of suitable prospects on your behalf from information you provide about the type of customers you're looking for.

Making the Most of Your Mailing List

Once you've put some graft into building up a customer mailing list, keeping the list in good order enables you to get the best results from it. This section looks at how to store the information you gather, as well as how to enhance it.

REMEMBER

However you choose to store and use your customer information, you'll need to abide by certain legal requirements. Check out the section 'Keeping Your Records Legal' for more on this.

Storing customer information

Once you've got your customer information, you need to put it together in such a way that it can be used for mailings. Also, you need to store it in a single location to make it more accessible.

Old technology or new?

Using paper records is a good idea:

- If you have a small list
- If you intend to keep your mailings small

Using a computer database to store your records is better:

- If you have a larger customer base
- If your list is expanding rapidly
- If you want to run a more sophisticated mailing programme

TRY THIS

Planning a customer questionnaire

Draw up a list of categories you'd like to collect data about for each of your customers. Against each category specify how you'd use the information, as well as what sources you could use to get it, both internal and external.

There are two key ways to store information:

- On paper
- On a computer

It may sound positively prehistoric but starting off by using paper records is perfectly acceptable. However, if you really want to make the most of your mailings in the future, it's a good idea to think about getting all this customer information in an electronic format. It's much easier and less time-consuming to manage any data on a computer.

Take a look at the sidebar 'Old technology or new?' to judge which alternative you should opt for initially.

Collecting more than names and addresses

When it comes to gathering useful information about your customers, don't stop with names and addresses. Get as much data as you can about their buying habits, their home environments, marital status, if they have children, and so on. All this information allows you to target your mailing more effectively, and to send particular offers to specific customers. For example, if you can work out who your best customers are, you could devise a mailing just for them. But remember, all the information you collect must be relevant to your business and obtained fairly and legally.

EXAMPLE

Figure 4-2 shows a couple of sample checklists, to make sure you're getting the right sort of information:

REMEMBER

Depending on the nature of your business, you might need more specialist information (for example, a car tyre company needs to know the make and model), but don't be put off if you don't have this information, you can run a successful mailing with simple names and addresses.

Consumer checklist
Title
Surname
First name/initials
Address
Postcode
Daytime/evening telephone numbers
Age bracket
Income brand
Purchase history – dates, values, products bought
Credit/payment/debit record
Children – number, sexes, ages, first names
Marital status

Business checklist
Company name
Address
Postcode
Telephone number
Fax number
Email address
Key contact name(s)
Job title(s)
Type of business (SIC code*)
Location
Number of employees
Business turnover

Figure 4-2: Examples of consumer and business checklists.

Keeping Your Records Legal

Chapter 14 goes into more detail about the legal aspects of direct mailing, but for the purposes of keeping customer records and contacting potential new customers, this section gives you the basics you need to know.

Strict penalties are enforced for failing to comply with the Data Protection Act 1998, so if you are in doubt about the legitimacy of your database, take advice from The Information Commissioner, Wycliffe House, Water Lane, Wilmslow, SK9 5AF. Tel: 01625 545 745.

It must be clear to people what you are intending to use their data for, plus they must have the option to say whether or not you can use the data for those purposes, and that you must stop mailing them if they request it. Don't think of this as a negative; if someone doesn't want to receive your mailing, you'd be wasting valuable time and resources sending it to them, when it could go to someone else more receptive. The information you keep must also be accurate and up to date.

An example of compliance with the Data Protection Act is the following extract (you could include this in your mailing):

> *From time to time we send out promotional material about our products and services. If you don't want to receive it, please tick the following box:* ❑

Get in touch with the Mailing Preference Service (Tel: 020 7738 1625; Web: `www.mpsonline.org.uk`) for updated information about those members of the public who have opted not to receive direct mail. It's a very reasonably priced resource for small businesses. Additionally, contact OFCOM (The Office of Communications) (Tel: 020 7981 3000; Web: `www.ofcom.org.uk`) for more information about restrictions applying to direct marketing by telephone and fax.

Chapter 5

Getting Your Customers to Respond

In This Chapter

- Gaining your audience's interest
- Encouraging your audience to respond
- Estimating response rates
- Sending mailings at the right time

In this chapter we take a look at the all important area of response and most important of all, how to boost it.

Discovering What Makes Your Audience Respond

For your mailshot to be successful, you need people to take notice of what you're sending to them. You can pique people's interest in your products or services through a few tried and tested methods.

REMEMBER

To make any direct mail campaign a success, you should be tapping into two emotions:

- **Self-interest:** For example, 'Why can't shops stock more of your size?'
- **The need for news:** Such as, 'Now you can get rid of aphids forever!'

Remember Your Mailing Objectives

Objectives are really crucial to any direct mail campaign. Remind yourself what you want to achieve with your mailing (see Chapter 3 for more on this). Whatever they are, make sure your offer supports your objectives. If you get this part of the planning stage right, you're halfway there.

People take notice if they can:

- Make money
- Save money
- Save time and effort
- Help their families
- Feel more comfortable or secure
- Impress others
- Gain pleasure
- Improve themselves
- Feel part of a group
- Feel they are doing good for others (for example, by giving to charity)

Try to combine two or more of these motivations in your offer to make an even stronger case for your product or service.

Don't promise the world, but you can offer to:

- **Provide the solution to a specific problem:** In the 'Here it is, the product you've been waiting for . . .' vein.
- **Guarantee quality:** Make sure you can substantiate the 'best ever' claim, of course!
- **Guarantee value.** Again, make sure you can substantiate the 'Best price' claim.
- **Availability:** 'We have it in stock . . .', possibly when others don't.

- **A free trial or demonstration:** Home or office trials can be very effective, and mailings offering such deals convince potential customers you have faith in your product.
- **Provide reassurance:** A testimonial from an existing satisfied customer adds extra credibility to your offer.

Deciding What to Include in Your Mailshot

You can include many different items in a mailshot, but think about each one beforehand: What role does it play and why are you including it?

The most common choices of content are:

- A letter
- A brochure or catalogue
- A flyer
- A gift voucher
- A business reply envelope/card

The next three sections look at using the first three of these in combination.

Sending just a letter

Sometimes a letter is all you need for a successful mailshot. So long as you give your customer a way of responding, a letter can do the job nicely. Send a letter if you want to achieve the following:

- You want to welcome or thank a customer
- You're sending a promotional offer (such as an invitation to an event) to existing customers
- Your offer is easy to explain

Sending a letter and a brochure

You might want to include a brochure or catalogue as well as a letter if:

- You want to show off your full product range
- You want customers to order over the telephone or by post
- Your product is visually appealing so you want to include a vivid image
- You're mailing a new customer and you want to provide them with more information

Sending a letter and a flyer

A flyer can give you extra space to tell your story. Include one alongside your letter if:

- You don't need a brochure but the chance to recap all your key sales points would help
- There's not enough room in your letter to cover all the relevant details
- You want to use it to include testimonials from existing customers

Describing Your Products and Services

If you want to best describe your product or services, find out what makes your product or service special by asking yourself the following questions:

- How does my product or service differ from my competitors'? Is it better, for example, or more affordable?
- Why would someone want my product or services? What are the benefits?

Playing around with your ideas

To get some practice in before committing to a real life mailshot, try your ideas out in the following way:

1. Choose one of your products or services and analyse its strengths and weaknesses.
2. Make a list of its key features and explain how each of these can benefit the people who buy it. State why it's better than your competitors' product or service.
3. Now imagine you're developing a mailshot to promote this product. Write down, in a single sentence, why a customer would want to buy it.

- Is my product or service a replacement for a previous one? What improvements have been made?
- Is there something special about my product or services' background or production to interest potential customers?

Focus on the benefits of a product, not on its features. *Features* are technical information that the customer may not want to know, but *benefits* are ways in which the customer's life is going to get easier or better. Benefits are your key selling tools. For example, if you're selling a vacuum cleaner that weighs only 8 lbs, the '8 lbs' is a feature, while a benefit is that it's lightweight and therefore easier to use.

All advertisements need to be legal, decent, and truthful, in accordance with the Committee of Advertising Practice (CAP); this applies to direct mail as well. Copies of the code as well as free, confidential advice are available from the Advertising Standards Authority (see Chapter 14 for more details).

Understanding How Different Offers Affect Responses

Presenting an offer as part of your direct mail campaign can produce a better response rate. Such offers fall into a number of different categories:

- Those that generate high-volume response (such as: enquiry invitations)
- Those that generate high-quality response (such as: repeat purchase offers)
- Those that generate maximum short-term sales (such as: discount offers)
- Those that generate long-term gains (such as: loyalty offers)

Getting the response rate you desire

Think about what you're trying to achieve before you decide what sort of offer to make (and therefore which response you'll get). So, for example, are you trying to:

- Increase the number of people on your mailing list? If so, you want lots of responses.
- Generate sales leads? If yes, you'll want high-quality responses.
- Hit a sales target? In this case, you'll want as many people as possible to buy – maybe offer an incentive.
- Secure the longer term success of your business? If so, you'll want to focus on customer loyalty.

Boosting response rates

The best way to boost response is to offer an incentive. An *incentive* is an inducement for your prospect to act. You can offer anything as an incentive, but the more relevant it is to your business, the better it will work for you.

Here's some incentive ideas:

- Free gift
- Competition or a free prize draw
- A discount of some kind – like 'two for one'
- Temporary price reduction

- Volume discount (for example, 10 per cent off a bulk purchase)
- Low or no interest
- 'Buy now, pay later'
- Early-bird incentive (for example, a free gift for replying within a certain time)
- Seasonal or end-of-line sales
- Voucher
- 'Buy one, get one free' offer

REMEMBER

Don't forget to include any price reductions or incentives in your budget and break-even figures when you're calculating them (see Chapter 3 for more on this).

Just like advertising, sales promotions need to be legal, decent and truthful to comply with the Code of Sales Promotion, a code of practice policed by the Advertising Standards Authority (www.asa.org.uk). It's an offence to give misleading pricing information – there's a Code of Practice for Traders on Price Indications that you also have to comply with when advertising prices – especially special promotions or sale prices. Chapter 14 gives more details on staying legal.

Offering a response device

You must always give your customers a way to reply to your offer (a *response device*) – partly so you can deal with their response (which might be an order!) but also so you can gain other information about them. The choice of response devices includes: reply paid cards, telephone numbers, fax numbers, Web pages, and e-mail addresses.

TIP

If you include a response coupon, make sure you:

- Request all the relevant customer details you need for your offer and your mailing list.
- Include a request for payment details, if appropriate.
- Include an individual code so you can track the response to your mailing.
- Make the response card easy to fill in.

- Enclose a reply-paid envelope or freepost address to make it easier to return – or give customers a range of options to respond: such as by coupon, phone, Web, e-mail, or fax.
- Include Data Protection information to ensure your mailing stays within the law.

Sending Your Mailshot at the Right Time

The best time to mail a customer is when they're in the market for your product or service. But how do you find out when this time is? Here are some ideas:

- Does your product have any seasonality in its sales cycle? Okay, if you're selling Easter eggs or Christmas decorations, you've probably worked out the best time to market them, but seasonality can be present to a lesser extent in other products too – BBQ food in summer, for example, or garden furniture in spring.
- Do your customers renew their product at a particular time of year? Insurance is a good example of this – if you don't know when someone's policy is up, you've got a one in 12 chance of mailing them at a relevant time. Why not use a mailing initially to find out when their insurance expires and then use the information for another mailing later on?
- Can you tie in your mailing with some other activity? For example, a decorator may target people who have just moved house, or a travel agents may contact people just after they've returned from holiday and their (hopefully good) experience is still fresh in their minds.

Chapter 6

Getting the Best from Your Customers

In This Chapter

- Finding out why developing customer relationships is a good thing
- Identifying your best customers and their needs
- Keeping your customers loyal
- Using existing customers to get new ones

You shouldn't ignore the evidence: time and again, studies show that concentrating on existing customers generates more profit, more quickly, than setting off into unknown territory to find new ones. Look after your customers, and they look after you.

REMEMBER

If you lose a customer to your competition, it can cost you up to six times more to replace her with a new one. That's why you need to hang on to the customers you have and encourage their loyalty. It's also vitally important to understand who your most profitable customers are.

Here are a few ideas about building customer loyalty and profitability:

- Give existing profitable customers plenty of T.L.C.
- Contact them regularly
- Listen to what they tell you
- Exceed their expectations
- Resolve any complaints quickly and effectively

For your current customers consider using the ideas from the following list:

- Devise five opportunities to write to your customer that would strengthen your relationships with them.
- Write a sample questionnaire asking for feedback after a customer purchase.
- Plan a *customer-get-customer scheme* for your business, spreading goodwill to increase your customer base. How would you work out which customers to target? What incentives would you use to encourage them to introduce potential customers?

Finding Out Who Your Best Customers Are

Almost every company finds that the bulk of their business comes from a minority of customers – it's called the *80/20 rule,* which means 80 per cent of your business comes from 20 per cent of your customers.

You can see how important it is to identify these people; the following list suggests some ways to pick them out:

- Customer sales records should give you a pretty good idea of who's spending what with your business, how often, and on what.
- If you don't keep sales records (for example, you own a shop), you still might remember who's face you see most regularly and how much he spends on what products.
- Hold events, run competitions, create questionnaires; get to know your customers and stay in touch.

Giving them the red carpet treatment

Looking after your best customers is definitely worth it when you consider that research shows that this top 20 per cent:

- Pays more for your products than less loyal customers
- Buys more products than less loyal customers
- Costs less to administer
- Costs less to advertise to

The idea behind customer loyalty is not to lavish attention on 20 per cent who buy with you and neglect the remaining 80 per cent who buy with you; the idea is to turn all of your customers into your best, and most loyal customers, who are prepared to recommend your business to their family and friends.

Knowing what they want

The key to knowing what customers want is to ask them . . . and then to listen very carefully to their reply. Here are some ways of finding out exactly what your customers *do* want:

- A questionnaire following up a customer purchase
- A research survey about potential new products and services
- A telephone call to find out about satisfaction or any problems with a particular product
- A discussion group to debate new or existing products

Keeping Customers Loyal

The good news is you can use mailshots to increase customer loyalty. Here are just some of the ways you can do so:

- Welcome them to your company
- Thank them for a purchase
- Encourage them to buy goods or services that complement something they've already bought
- Remind them to renew service contracts
- Make them feel involved by letting them know about developments at your company – such as new product lines or services

Five mailshots you can write in a couple of hours

Here's a few ideas to help you build loyalty – they're often overlooked, but they're quick, simple, and cheap:

- **'Thank you'.** After a purchase, write to your customer to say thank you and encourage them to get in touch if there's any problem. If you can suggest any additional products or services that might be of interest to them, even better, but remember to keep them relevant to the customer concerned.
- **'Thought I should let you know . . .'.** If you have news that's relevant to some or all of your customers, drop them a line to let them know. For example: 'We're holding a special preview sale where you'll get an extra 20 per cent off'; 'There's a new upgrade . . .'; 'We've introduced a new service . . .'; 'In July, we're moving to . . .'.
- **'Seasons Greetings'.** Holidays are an ideal opportunity to send your customers your best wishes. But remember, your customers may come from many different cultural and religious backgrounds, so keep your message non-denominational.
- **'Just a quick reminder . . .'.** Many people buy products requiring regular servicing or that are under warranty. When the warranty is about to expire, contact them – not only will your mail serve as a timely and thoughtful reminder, it also gives you the opportunity to communicate with them about new or other products and services.
- **'Please come back to us . . .'.** *Lapsed customers* are those that have bought from you in the past but no longer do. These people are important to your business too and a mailshot is a good way to reactivate people. Offers or new product launches are ideal for this type of mailshot, but bear in mind the customer might have left because of bad service, so consider including an 'If we have offended you . . .' apology.

- Send them special invitations to 'valued customer' events
- Send them best wishes for Christmas or an anniversary

The most important words in marketing are not 'new', 'first', or 'best', they are 'thank you'.

Real customer loyalty is born out of deep-seated beliefs in the values of a product or organisation. Factors such as quality, credibility, and integrity are mainstays of building customer loyalty. If your products or businesses lack these, offering incentives or discounts only delivers temporary loyalty to you.

Increasing customer loyalty in other ways

In addition to mailshots, you can increase customer loyalty through several other approaches. Here are a quartet of ideas (and check out Chapter 7 for some more tips):

- **Newsletters.** Newsletters provide a perfect opportunity to keep your customers up to date with what's happening in your company and in your industry – but with no (direct!) pressure to buy anything. They're usually published on a quarterly or bi-annual basis so are a good way of keeping you firmly in your customers' minds. Royal Mail produces a booklet entitled *How to produce a company newsletter;* give them a call on 0345 950 950 to request one.
- **Customer clubs.** Another way to build loyalty is to develop a club for regular customers. The secret to a club's success is making people feel as though they belong. Why not:
  - Invite customers to join the club but position your invite as a 'thank you' for their long-term custom.
  - Explain the benefits of belonging to the club, such as exclusive offers and sales previews.
  - Mail club members regularly to remind them how valuable they are to you. Position all offers as 'Exclusive to club members'.
  - Produce a club membership card or loyalty card that rewards the customer with discounts.
  - Publish a customer magazine for club members.
- **After sales service.** A follow-up call to a customer to make sure she's happy with her purchase, knows how to use it, and isn't experiencing any difficulties is a great way to ensure customer satisfaction.

- **Complaints.** It's a funny thing, but research shows that customers who have had a complaint resolved satisfactorily are more inclined to purchase from your company again than customers who have never had cause to complain. Customers who complain expect to:
  - Receive a prompt, personal apology, with someone taking responsibility.
  - Be offered a fair solution.
  - See that the company cares and is understanding.
  - Be offered a goodwill gesture in addition to any compensation due.
  - Receive a follow up to check the problem has been resolved.

Keeping your customers sweet

Just as it's easy to start building customer loyalty, damaging loyalty is just as easy. Two simple – but unfortunately common – pitfalls to avoid are:

- **Misspelling a customer's name and/or address.** This sort of carelessness reflects badly on you, your company, and your products.
- **Getting a customer's history wrong.** Remembering what products a customer has bought, when you last saw them, and so on is a way of showing you care. Get it right and your customer feels like you're taking a real interest in them, get it wrong and your customer could lose confidence and go elsewhere.

Chapter 7

Using Direct Mail Alongside Other Approaches

In This Chapter

- Using other advertising methods in conjunction with direct mail
- Planning your multi-channel campaign
- Making sure your approach to customers is 'joined up'

In this chapter we look at other approaches you can take to communicate with your customer, which can work well with direct mail.

A strategy that includes lots of different approaches, is known as a *multi-channel* strategy. The important thing about a multi-channel strategy is that the different types of customer communication need to work well together, rather than pulling the customer – and your business! – in different directions. That's why we've called this a *joined up* approach – your right hand really needs to know what your left hand is doing!

Using Other Advertising Alongside Direct Mail

This section lists some examples of different approaches and how they can be used to complement a direct mail campaign.

Unaddressed leafleting

This approach is also known as *door-to-door*. It has many of the same advantages as mailshots, which is why the whole of Chapter 8 of this book is devoted to it (flick through to that chapter for more info). Make sure that you're not simply duplicating your message by combining this approach with direct mail.

Press ads

Placing ads in newspapers and magazines could either generate sales or, at the very least, sales leads. You can then follow these up with a direct mail campaign, referring people to the press ad and encouraging them to take the action you require.

Of course, the publication you place your ad in depends on who you're trying to attract. For examples, check out Table 7-1.

Table 7-1 Choosing the Correct Publication to Advertise In

Your goal	*Where to advertise*
I'm trying to attract local people	Local newspapers
I'm looking to attract a wider audience	Regional newspapers
I want to attract people with a particular interest/hobby	Specialist magazines. Visit the reference section of your local library or look in *BRAD* (a listing of all UK publications that also provides circulation figures and reader profiles)
I want to advertise to other businesses in a particular industry	Trade magazines. Again, *BRAD* has a listing or you could contact the relevant trade organization

Local directories

People often turn to a business directory first – usually the *Yellow Pages* or *Thomson Local* – when they're looking for a product or service, so it makes sense to advertise here. When conducting a direct mail campaign, you could refer to the fact that you advertise in, for example, the *Yellow Pages,* so that your prospect always knows where to find your details.

Radio ads

This can be a cost-effective way of reaching both local and larger audiences. You can get a response if you include a phone number or Freepost name in the ad. You could back up your radio advertising with a direct mail campaign referring to the radio ad in the mailing piece.

'Piggy-back' inserts

Nothing to do with farming, these are leaflets and flyers that you include when sending everyday correspondence to your customer (such as invoices and account statements). Piggy-back inserts are cost-effective but they have to be relevant to the particular customer to be successful.

TIP: Banks and utilities companies use this technique a lot. Next time you get your statement or bill, have a look to see what they've included and what works for you.

REMEMBER: If someone has stated they don't want to receive unsolicited materials, you can't include inserts alongside other correspondence.

Telemarketing

Telemarketing can be really effective (particularly outbound telephone sales work) especially when targeted at existing customers. Make sure:

- **You have a valid reason for calling.** For instance, a tie-in with an offer you have publicised by direct mail. You might call to enquire if your customer received your mailing.

- **You have a solid reputation.** The telephone is a very personal and intrusive way of communicating, so make sure there is a good reason for your call. This way you will ensure all future calls are welcomed by your customers.
- **You consider the timing of your call.** Check the Direct Marketing Association's Code of Practice for guidelines as to when you can make calls. See their Web site: `www.dma.org.uk` for more details.

  Telephone calls are more intrusive than mailshots so always handle outbound telemarketing with care.
- **Your calls are properly structured, managed, and legal.** This makes the call more effective, so:
  - Get your telemarketers to follow an outline script to ensure they cover all key selling points.
  - Make sure they're sufficiently trained to overcome customers' objections.
  - Make sure they have a sound knowledge of the product or service.

Why not use outbound telemarketing to follow up a mailing and stir up non-respondents? Research shows that following up a mailing with a phone call increases response!

Planning Out Your Joined Up Approach

Before diving headlong into a joined up advertising campaign, take a bit of time to:

- Draw up a list of potential newspapers and magazines where you could advertise. Give your reasons for choosing them. Remember your objectives.
- Think of other methods you could use to advertise your products or services. Make a list and note the strengths and weaknesses of each.

Successfully Joining Up Your Campaign

TIP

Follow these four hints to make your joined up approach a success:

- **Set your objectives.** Ask yourself what you're trying to achieve. To raise awareness? Testing demand for a new product? Or are you trying to boost sales?
- **Define your targets.** Never forget who you are talking to. This way you'll make good decisions about which combination of approaches to use.
- **Be consistent.** Make sure your message and look (your *image or branding*) is consistent across all aspects of your campaign.
- **Measure the results.** Give every press ad, coupon, and mailshot a separate code so you can measure how effectively each element is working for you.

Chapter 8

Distributing Door Drops

In This Chapter

- Assessing the pros of door drops
- Weighing up the cons of door drops
- Working out how to distribute door drops

Door drops means distributing flyers, brochures, and other advertising material to homes and businesses without addressing them to a particular person. As the pieces do not have an address on them, they are delivered to an area rather than an individual.

This chapter looks at the good and bad of the door drop approach, and also outlines the basic methods of distributing in this way.

Realising the Advantages of Door Drops

First the good news: Door drops bring with them a lot of advantages. You can:

- Reach a wide audience
- Target customers according to location
- Acquire new customers
- Build a database

Door drop distribution is particularly effective for two marketing methods – the inclusion of coupons and free samples. The following two sections consider these options.

Including coupons

Redemption coupons (coupons that can be exchanged for money off or discounts) are very popular with door drop advertisers. Research shows that door drop redemption levels are 4.5 per cent compared with the one or two per cent redemption rate for coupons placed in magazines.

Redemption coupons:

- Are a good way to trigger sales
- Prompt customers to switch to another brand
- Are often kept or passed on
- Can provoke a quick response, if you limit the time the offer is valid for

Offering samples

Door drops give you the chance to offer your customer the chance to try out your product. If an item fits in through the letterbox and is non-toxic, there's no reason not to send customers a sample (though it's clearly not a good idea for highly perishable goods). For example:

- A garden nursery could send a packet of seeds
- A stationer could send a pen
- An events organiser could send a packet of balloons
- A caterer could send a packet of birthday cake candles

Spotting the Disadvantages of Door Drops

Alongside the benefits of door drops, a few drawbacks are worth considering. For instance:

- You can't personalise your material for a specific individual
- You can't target as accurately – targeting postcode sectors rather than individuals
- It's more difficult to use door drops for business mailings
- Door drops are not suitable to products that only appeal to a niche market

Distributing Door Drops

If you decide that door drops are right for your direct mail campaign, several ways of implementing your mailing may be used:

- Organising your own distribution (great for small areas)
- Using an independent distributor
- Delivering via a free newspaper (the promotional piece is delivered with the newspaper but not as an insert)
- Using Royal Mail (the items are delivered with the rest of the post by the postman)

TRY THIS

Thinking door drops

Try these tasks before committing to a door drop campaign:

- Think of three uses of door drops for your organisation
- Write down any sampling ideas you have; if you can't send your actual product through the post, is there anything else you could send that would make people think about your product?

Chapter 9

Testing Your Mailshot's Effectiveness

In This Chapter

- Making your mailshot more effective
- Checking for errors and fixing them
- Carrying out your tests methodically

One of the best things about direct mail is that it's easy and cheap to work out what's effective and what's not. This chapter looks at the means available to you for *testing* – checking on, modifying, and improving the mailshots you send.

Improving Your Mailshot

If you're looking to make your mailshot even better, look at these five basics to test (we've listed them in order of importance):

- **The audience:** Are you sending your mailing to the right people?
- **The offer:** Are you promoting the right products? Could you incorporate a special incentive?
- **The timing:** Are you sending your mailing at the right time?
- **The response device:** Are you asking people to respond in the right way?
- **The creative approach:** Is your mailshot well presented?

These five factors are covered in the following sections.

Hitting the correct audience

REMEMBER

Accurate targeting is the biggest factor determining the success or failure of your mailshot. The more precise your targeting, the better. No one ever got rich trying to sell lawnmowers to people living in flats, or cars to people who don't drive!

TIP

Use a *sample* (a small section of your list), to judge what your responses will be like before you roll out the entire mailshot.

Possible sample groups include:

- Existing customers
- Enquirers
- Lapsed customers
- Purchased or cold lists

Testing offers

When testing an offer, think back to your objectives (see Chapter 3 for ideas on this). The type of incentive you include could impact not only response, but what happens next. For example, a free gift may encourage lots of responses but not necessarily get people buying. Other test options might include:

- Incentives and freebies
- Payment terms
- Payment options
- Guarantees
- Price discounts
- Speed premiums

Getting the timing right

Timing is often neglected in tests but is an important factor in success. Many products, other than the obvious – Easter eggs and fireworks, for example – have seasonal cycles. Timing test options include:

- Day in the month
- Month
- Season

Testing response mechanisms

Though the response method you offer (for example, e-mail address, coupon, or telephone number) can have a big impact on the success of your mailshot, it's generally unnecessary to test these methods separately because you can incorporate a choice in your mailshot.

Just because one response method proves more popular than others, don't be tempted to reduce the choice. Often, more people respond precisely because they have a choice.

Balancing your creativity

Test both the physical format of your mailing (for example, size or number of elements enclosed), and the creative approach (for example, font and layout). Both have a role to play, but research shows that these factors influence response less than the others (audience, offer, timing, response device).

The key to testing creative treatments is not to overdo it. Options for testing include:

- Emphasis
- Envelope style
- Headlines
- Length of copy
- Number of elements
- Shape
- Size

Knowing What to Tweak . . . and When to Tweak It!

To make the most of your test, consider the following list of hints and tips:

- **Test one thing at a time.** If you change more than one aspect of your mailing, you won't be able to tell which one affected response.
- **Give your test variant a separate code.** Coding enables you to work out which responses are from the test mailing and which are from the *controlled mailing* (the mailing pack against which your response is being measured).
- **Test more than once.** Don't rely on the outcome of a single test – repeat it several times.
- **Test big changes rather than small.** For example, a test pack with or without an incentive, rather than a 10 per cent discount instead of a 12 per cent discount.
- **Act quickly on your test results.** If your test produces an *actionable result* (something you can incorporate in your next mailing) act on it as soon as possible, before circumstances change.

Putting Your Tests into Practice

The simplest testing of your mailshot is the *split test*, whereby you compare one set of conditions against another.

Here's a step-by-step guide to conducting your own split test:

1. **Establish your objective.** What do you want to find out from the test? For example, working out whether a product appeals more to one group of customers than another. When you've decided, work out a way of testing for it.
2. **Establish your control.** Your *control* should be your best performing mailshot; use this as a yardstick against which to measure your test results.

3. **Plan your test.** Select a sample of names from your customer list and divide it in two: control and test. Limit your test to a small fraction of your total list – no more than 30 per cent.

   If testing different target audiences, select random samples from the appropriate lists.

4. **Conduct your test.** Remember, all test conditions must remain consistent bar one, to make it clear how that one factor affects the mailshot.

   Code your response devices, otherwise you won't be able to tell which are from the control group and which are from the test group.

5. **Analyse your results.** A clear difference in results (for example, one per cent compared to 10 per cent) speaks for itself. If the difference is marginal, repeat the test to see if you can achieve a more definitive result.

If you're testing an incentive, make sure the increase in response justifies the cost.

Part III

Writing and Designing Successful Mailshots

'It says here, you are artistic and have a good knowledge of typefaces — Do you have any samples handy?'

In this part . . .

Here's the creative bit of the book . . . this part gifts you with loads of practical advice for writing and designing effective mailshots. Beauty may be in the eye of the beholder, and presentation might not make or break your mailing, but a good-looking, well-written letter or brochure can certainly pay dividends.

Chapter 10

Writing a Successful Mailshot

In This Chapter

- Writing effective letters for different reasons
- Getting the envelope just right
- Writing additional material to include with a letter
- Creating the best response device
- Developing questionnaires

You've gathered together information on what you think makes for a good mailshot, sorted out your goals and target audience, and organised your direct mail database to make sure you reach the right people. Now what? Well, making sure that your direct mail campaign is written to appeal to your audience is a good step forward! This chapter points you in the right direction for getting your wording just as you need it.

Writing Your Letter Creatively

If your mailshot wrote itself, this step would be just that little bit easier . . . but as it won't write itself, this section contains our advice on getting things just right (or write).

How do I write an effective sales letter?

With a little practice you should be able to turn out your sales letter you include in your mailshot in about 30 minutes.

Simply ask yourself the following questions and arrange the answers in letter form:

- **Do you have the name of your customer?** If so, address the letter to them. If you know them well, use their first name. If not, use their title and surname. If you don't have their name, use a default greeting – 'Dear reader' or 'Dear gardener'.
- **What's your main reason for writing?** What are you offering your customer?
- **Why is it of benefit to them?**
- **Are there any other benefits for the customer?**
- **Can you offer your customer a guarantee that this is the right product for them?**
- **Can you encourage your customer to respond more quickly?**
- **Is there any information they will need to respond?**
- **Have you signed the letter?** Use your full name.
- **Ask yourself again: Is there any way to encourage your customer to respond or can you restate your main benefit?**

Figure 10-1 shows an example of an effective sales letter.

How do I make my letter easy to read and understand?

Follow the advice in this list to help keep your letter simple and understandable:

- **Use short sentences.** 16 words is a good general rule; don't exceed 32 words.
- **Use short paragraphs.** Limit each paragraph to one thought or idea.
- **Concentrate on style.** A good way to write is to write as you would speak.
- **Minimise punctuation.** Over punctuation can be . . . confusing!

	B&D Garden Supplies Apple Blossom Lane FLORAL TOWN POSTCODE
Customer name not known – use default greeting	Dear Gardener 17th Month 1999
Main offer or benefit	In July, you can save 25% on any model from the Hover Mower range at B&D Garden Supplies.
Expansion of main benefit	And with prices starting from as little as £65.00, you can see how affordable it is to treat yourself to a quality new mower this summer.
Other reasons to buy the product	But price isn't the only reason you would want to buy a Hover Mower. Their lightweight design makes them easy to manoeuvre, even over uneven lawns, and a safety cut-out means you never have to worry if you accidentally catch the lead. There's a durable cutting blade too, made from high tensile tungsten, which just goes on and on and on. Hover Mower models are built to last which means you'll enjoy your Hover Mower for years to come.
Product reassurance – popularity and guarantee	All these benefits make it easy to see why so many of our customers choose Hover Mowers. In fact, they account for over 75% of our lawnmower sales. And with a 5-year guarantee on parts and labour, you can be confident that you're making the right choice.
What makes the company special	If you're not sure which Hover Mower will suit your needs best, don't worry. One of our expert staff is always on hand to advise you.
Information which will enable and encourage the customer to respond	We're open Monday to Friday 9am to 6pm and on Saturday from 9am to 5pm. There's customer parking at the rear of the centre and we can also arrange free delivery of any large items.
Offer end date to encourage quick response	But remember, the 25% discount is only available until the end of July so hurry down to the garden centre today.
	I look forward to seeing you there.
	Yours sincerely,
	Jack Jones
	Jack Jones
Added incentive to boost response	P.S. Please accept this voucher for a free sachet of Mow-well lawn feed which you can collect when you visit our garden centre.

Figure 10-1: An effective sales letter.

- **Be warm and friendly.** Let your personality shine through but don't be over familiar.
- **Count the 'you' word.** 'You' is a very important word; it should appear at least two or three times more often than 'I', 'we', or 'our'.
- **Use everyday words and phrases.** Big words can sound grandiloquent, bombastic, and orotund (that's pompous to you or to me; see what we mean?).
- **Use superlatives sparingly.** Words like 'fabulous', 'marvelous', and 'amazing' don't really convince anyone.

Six things to do once you've finished writing

As any good editor will tell you, before sending your masterpiece out, be sure to:

- Check spelling and grammar
- Ask someone to read your letter aloud to see how it flows
- Check the letter begins with your main point
- Look out for any distractions (such as information relevant to other products but not the one you're mailing about)
- Get other people's input
- Give your letter the 'overnight test' and read it again the following day. If it still reads well, send it.

TIP

Get straight to the point. Don't waste time at the start of the letter introducing yourself or your business, you can do that later. Tell the customer straight away what's in it for them.

How do I overcome writer's block?

Getting started is often the hardest part of writing. We offer the following ideas to get going, or to keep up the momentum if you're starting to flag:

- Hold an imaginary conversation with your customer and write down everything you'd say face-to-face.
- Hold an imaginary conversation as suggested in the previous bullet, but try recording it on a tape recorder.
- Allow yourself plenty of time to write your letter.
- Work out when your most productive time is and write during that time.
- Write down all your ideas – whether you think they're good, bad, or indifferent – and select the best (sometimes your opinions change when you've got them down in writing).
- Write more than you need to, then edit it down.

25 ways to begin a letter

The first three or four words are potentially the most important of your mailshot . . . and are also the most difficult to write. Here are some suggested openings:

- 'Ask yourself – where would . . .'
- 'Did you ever see . . .'
- 'Do you know . . .'
- 'Have you ever felt . . .'
- 'How would you like . . .'
- 'How many times have you . . .'
- 'Here's the free . . .'
- 'I believe you are . . .'
- 'I trust . . .'
- 'I want to thank you . . .'
- 'If I came into your home/office . . .'
- 'If my letter has . . .'
- 'If you could . . .'
- 'I'm delighted to . . .'
- 'Let me ask you – what if . . .'
- 'Most people never expect . . .'
- 'Since we last . . .'
- 'The fact is, if you're . . .'
- 'This is your chance to . . .'
- 'Who do you call . . .'
- 'Would you like to . . .'
- 'Wouldn't it be . . .'
- 'You could be . . .'
- 'You don't have to be a . . .'
- 'You're not on your own if . . .'

How do I judge if my letter will be a success?

Keeping a few ideas in your mind about what your readers will think when they read your mailshot helps to make sure that your letter hits its objective.

Here's a simple checklist of common thoughts to help you assess your letter:

- Who are you and why are you writing to me?
- Can you prove what you're writing to me about? Where's the evidence?
- What's in it for me?
- What's so interesting about this?

Getting ready to write

Prepare yourself for writing a great mailshot by trying out these exercises first:

- Collect some mailings you've been sent and examine the creative techniques used. What are their good and bad points?
- Write a sample sales letter for one of your products. Review it against the criteria in the section 'How do I judge if my letter will be a success?'.
- Produce a simple questionnaire allowing you to collect more information about your customers.

- Who is this product or service for?
- Why are you writing to me?
- Why should I do it?
- What do you want from me?

How do I write a non-sales letter?

Lots of opportunities exist for writing letters that aren't specifically about sales, but that keep your customers happy and willing to buy from you again.

Examples of non-sales mailshots include:

- Thanking customers for repeat business
- Christmas or anniversary greetings
- Thanks for a specific purchase
- An important piece of company news
- Offering membership to a frequent buyer scheme

The secret of these kind of letters is:

- Keeping them short and sweet
- Making them personal to each customer
- Adding value when you can

- Keeping customers up to date with new developments
- Exploiting relevant anniversaries and seasonal opportunities

Choosing What to Put on the Envelope

Your envelope is important because it is the first impression the recipient gets of your company and it can make your letter stand out from the rest of the mail. Ask yourself: Will it encourage people to open it?

TIP: Consider who you're writing to. Make sure that however you choose to present your envelope it supports your objective. For example:

- **If you have a very strong offer or unique product, re-iterate this on your envelope.** Ideally, do this in a different way to the letter inside. Envelope messages that promise benefits are the best.
- **If you have important news, use an announcement style message on your envelope.** For example:
  - 'There's £50,000 on offer to one lucky reader'
  - 'Important news for arthritis sufferers'
- **If you want to make a 'surprising revelation', include a message on the envelope that stimulates people's curiosity.** Such tactics work well, for example:
  - 'What would you do with £50,000?'
  - 'Only open this envelope if you're prepared to be shocked!'

REMEMBER: Follow up curiosity headlines quickly, before interest drops off. And remember, what stimulates one person's curiosity could leave another customer cold, so follow up a curiosity headline with a benefit.

EXAMPLE: Figure 10-2 shows two curiosity headlines included on envelopes.

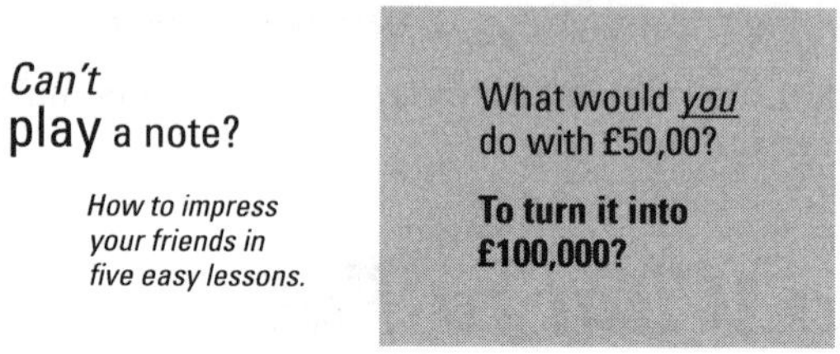

Figure 10-2: Messages on envelopes stimulate curiosity about the contents.

Writing Brochures and Leaflets

In addition to your mailshot letter, you might be thinking of writing a leaflet, brochure, or catalogue to accompany your letter. This section starts your creative juices flowing.

This section doesn't just apply to leaflets, even though that's the word we've used in this section. So wherever you see the word leaflet, think of it as shorthand for leaflets, brochures, catalogues, and pretty much any other type of material you're considering including in your mailshot along with your main letter.

How do I plan my leaflet effectively?

Follow these steps to create a great leaflet for your mailshot:

1. **Ask yourself why you are including a leaflet.** Do you want to:
    - Re-iterate all the key benefits of your product?
    - Explain your product in more detail?
    - Provide details of an entire range?
    - Highlight a limited offer promotion?
    - Present customer testimonials?

   - Provide background information on your company to help build its reputation?

   Remember that some mailshots work just as well with only a letter.

2. **Write a headline reflecting your objective.** Here are some examples:

   - 'All you need to know about "XXX" (your product)'
   - 'A comprehensive guide to our complete range of products'
   - 'Your chance to win a fabulous holiday for two in Jamaica'

3. **Gather all the source materials you need to write your leaflet.** These might include:

   - Technical specifications
   - Information on the product's history
   - Product reviews from magazines
   - Findings from customer research
   - Competitor mailings for similar products

4. **Sift through the information you've gathered and highlight any relevant points.** Use a highlighter pen and post-it notes to indicate the important pieces of information you've found.

5. **Write down, in bullet points, all the information you want to include.** When you've done so, arrange them into manageable chunks of text.

6. **You're ready to start writing your leaflet!**

How do I keep readers interested in my leaflet?

Take a look at the section entitled 'How do I make my letter easy to read and understand?' earlier in this chapter; what makes a letter great also makes a leaflet great. Additionally, check out these simple techniques to keep people reading your leaflet:

- Don't forget to caption pictures
- Keep repetition to a minimum
- Remember to include a call to action
- Use active words
- Use bullet points, numbered lists, and comparison tables
- Use link words and phrases – for example, start paragraphs with 'And', 'But', or 'What's more . . .'
- Use lots of headings and subheads to break up text
- Vary the pace of the text
- Write in the present tense wherever possible

Writing an Effective Response Device

A *response device* is something you supply to your prospect that, ideally, helps turn them into a customer. It's a method for them to reply, such as a paper or online order form, and the easier your response device is for them to use, the more chance they'll get it back to you.

TIP

Decide what information you want to include in your response device. You might want to collect the following:

- **Personal details.** Including: title (Mr, Mrs, and so on); gender; first name/s; surname; company name and position; postal address; phone number/s; e-mail address/es; and date of birth.

  If you already have some or all of these details you can use them to personalise your response device making it even easier for your customer to fill in.

- **Order and payment information if you want your customer to buy direct from the mailing.** You'll need to know: item; colour; quantity; and cost per item.

  You'll also need to include payment details. Options include: cash; cheque or postal order (specify who it should be made payable to); credit/debit card details; direct debit details.

Be aware that direct debit details are safeguarded by the Direct Debit Guarantee. Ask your bank for more details.

You might also want to use this opportunity to get some additional information, including: 'How often do you . . . ?'; 'When did you last . . . ?'; and, 'When is . . . due to expire?'

You must include an opt-out clause on your response device allowing respondents to indicate that they do not want to receive any further mailings from you.

Figure 10-3 shows a well thought-out response device.

Figure 10-3: A well thought-out response device.

Get a friend to fill out the response device and alert you to any difficulties they encounter.

Coming Up with a Questionnaire

When devising a questionnaire, be absolutely clear what will motivate your customer to fill it. If you expect to get something from your customers, you'll need to give them something in return. Also be clear about how the details you're requesting will benefit your business. Every answer should potentially give you insight into improving your mailshot.

Ask yourself what you need to know from your customers, remembering a good question should be:

- Clear and unambiguous
- Easy to respond to
- Easy to understand
- Relevant to the person being asked
- Relevant to your company's requirement for information

Avoiding common questionnaire pitfalls

The art of good questionnaire writing doesn't come easily to everyone. As a good starting point, remember these nuggets of advice:

- Avoid asking questions that are too trivial, too detailed, or require amazing feats of memory.
- Avoid asking two questions at once.
- Avoid leading questions such as, 'Did you hear about our company through our recent advertisement?'; 'Where did you hear about our company?' gives you more information.
- Avoid personal questions.
- Avoid using unfamiliar words or technical jargon.

REMEMBER

The more questions you ask the lower your response is likely to be. The number of responses might be a trade-off against depth of information.

Making sure the answers received are useful

Start off with *closed questions* (requiring a simple answer such as a straightforward 'Yes' or 'No'). Examples include, 'Do you own a washing machine?' and 'Do you watch satellite television?'

Giving people multiple choice answers is also useful and makes the questionnaire easier to complete. Figures 10-4 and 10-5 show two examples to base your own questionnaire on.

How satisfied are you with the service you receive from DL Motors?

Very satisfied ☐	Quite satisfied ☐	Neither satisfied or dissatisfied ☐
Quite dissatisfied ☐	Very dissatisfied ☐	

Figure 10-4: A 'tick the box' multiple choice questionnaire.

Please indicate how much you agree or disagree with the following statements (where 5 is strongly agree, 1 is strongly disagree). (Please circle the one that most closely reflects your opinion.)

RL Bakeries

Has an excellent product range	5	4	3	2	1
Provides exceptional service	5	4	3	2	1

Figure 10-5: A numerically-rated multiple choice questionnaire.

Providing clear and precise instructions about how to fill in the questionnaire makes it easier for respondents to fill the form in. For example, 'Please use block capitals' or 'Tick one box only'.

Chapter 11

Designing a Successful Mailshot

In This Chapter

- Creating an effective letter layout
- Putting together great leaflets
- Getting envelopes licked
- Making effective response devices
- Keeping costs down

Well thought-out objectives, enticing words, and great sales technique all help shape an effective direct mail campaign, but creating a mailshot that people want to pick up because of good design can be equally important. This chapter takes you through the basics.

Creating a Great Letter Layout

One of the keys to readability is making sure you use a legible typeface. Ideally your typeface should be *serif* (that is, having little tips and feet on the extremities of each letter – such as Times New Roman, Garamond, and Palatino), as research shows people generally find these easier to read than *sans serif* typefaces (without the tips and feet – such as Arial, Helvetica, and Verdana).

The typeface Times New Roman is often used in body copy because its wide setting makes it legible.

Another key to readability is the point size of the type. If it's too small people won't be able to read what you've written.

As a general rule, don't drop below point size 8 or run above point size 12 for body text; headings and 'small print' point sizes can vary, of course.

Some other ideas for creating great letter layouts include using:

- A box around your headline
- Bullet points and numerical lists
- Colour to highlight headings and subheads
- 'Hand-written' typefaces for added impact
- Indents for important paragraphs
- Italics, bold, and underlining

Using too many of the techniques listed in the preceding bullet list in the same letter can make things messy and lessen rather than increase impact.

If your letter runs over two pages, don't let the reader stop at the end of the page – make sure copy runs on, ideally in the middle of a really interesting sentence.

Putting Together a Leaflet, Brochure, or Catalogue

Many of the techniques described in the section 'Creating a Great Letter Layout' are relevant for leaflets. Even so, a few special design considerations specific to leaflets, brochures, and catalogues are also worth knowing about. Read on!

This section doesn't just apply to leaflets, even though that's the word we've used in this section. So wherever you see the word leaflet, think of it as shorthand for leaflets, brochures, catalogues, and pretty much any other type of material you're considering including in your mailshot along with your main letter.

When designing your own leaflet, follow these suggestions for achieving an effective layout:

- **Keep the front cover simple.** A single image or illustration with a single headline is probably the easiest and most effective cover to produce.

  What you put on the front cover should be inviting – it determines whether a potential customer will read on.

- **Decide on the number of columns.** This is the standard way that copy is laid out in, for example, magazines and newspapers. It's done to break up copy so you don't lose your place. Depending on how much copy you have, decide how many columns you want to use and how wide you want them to be.
- **Be consistent about columns.** Whatever layout you decide on, use the same number of columns on every page.
- **Don't be afraid of white space.** You don't have to fill all available space on your leaflet; white space can open up a design and is less overwhelming to the reader than banks of text.
- **Don't use reversed-out type for body copy.** *Reversed-out* copy is when, for example, white text is used on a black background. Research shows it can reduce comprehension by up to 70 per cent.
- **Put your headlines at the top.** This way, you'll achieve maximum impact.
- **Use text that is *justified* or *ranged left*.** This means that the text is lined up against the left-hand side of your page; it's much easier to read than ranged right text.

  Take a look at Figure 11-1 if you don't believe us that ranged right text is more difficult to read.

- **Limit the number of photographs or illustrations you use.** Too many can dilute impact.
- **Place pictures as near to headlines as possible.** Ideally, they should directly relate to one another.
- **Use size to indicate the importance of pictures.** The more important the picture, the bigger it should be.

Look at an existing brochure or leaflet – either your own or another company's. How easy is it to read? Are there any improvements you could make to the design? Use your findings in your own leaflet.

Top tips for successful photography

If you're including photos in your leaflet or letter, consider the following points:

- When taking photos avoid fussy backgrounds – they distract from the main image
- The best photos look unposed
- Make sure you use close-ups if including product shots
- Make sure you use close-ups if using shots of an individual person
- People in group shots are better arranged in crowds rather than lines

Figure 11-1: Justified or ranged left text is much easier to read than ranged right – see what we mean?

Deciding on Envelope Design

As outlined in Chapter 10, your envelope is just as important as its content. Here's a design checklist to help you get things right; ask yourself the following questions:

- Is the typeface easy to read?
- Would a coloured envelope help your mailing stand out from others?
- What about the address? Do you want it handwritten, stuck on as a printed label, or showing through an address window?

- If you've put a message on the envelope, does it stand out from a distance?
- Have you included an 'If undelivered, please return to . . .' line on the back?

Designing a Response Device

The most important thing to ask yourself about your response device is, 'Does the design make it easy to complete?' Here are some design suggestions to make sure the answer to the question is 'Yes':

- Leave plenty of space for answers.
- Use different colours to indicate where a response is required.
- Break down the form into questions.
- Provide an example of how to fill in potentially difficult areas of the form.
- State what to do next, including returning the response device (for example, if there's a business reply envelope, direct readers to it).
- Remember to include a response code so you can track the performance of your mailing.

Keeping Design Costs Down

Keep your costs down by design. The cost of your mailing can be made as low as possible by:

- Using only black, or black and one other colour (known as a *spot colour*)
- Producing your mailing in-house
- Reducing the number of items in your pack (for example, combine the letter and the response device onto one sheet)
- Keeping pictures and illustrations to a minimum

Chapter 12

Making the Most of Personalisation

In This Chapter

- Personalising mailings for your customers
- Using personal data in a creative fashion

Just as the name suggests, one of the best things about direct mail is that it allows you to talk directly to individual customers. The more personal you can make your message, the more likely it is to succeed.

Digital printing technology has made it even easier to personalise mailshots, so start by asking yourself what you know about your customer. Do you know:

- Their date of birth?
- Any renewal dates (for example, when their insurance expires)?
- Any special interest?
- Any order history?
- Any financial information/history?

Any of this information can be used to personalise mailings to your customers, and this chapter lends a helping hand.

TRY THIS

Examine an existing mailing you've sent out. How could you make more of the customer's name and address on this? Apply your findings to your next mailshot.

Making Mailings More Personal

You could personalise everything in your mailshot, but it's more common to personalise just the letter and response device (rather than leaflets, brochures, or anything else you're including).

A computer company sends a follow-up letter to customers thanking them for recent purchases. The framework of the letters is identical, but they add some important personal touches, as shown in Figure 12-1.

Sample Co
Sample Street
SAMPLE TOWN
POSTCODE

Dear [infill customer name] 17th Month 1999

Thank you for visiting our store on [infill date] and buying [infill product]. I hope you are pleased with your purchase and trust that everything is working satisfactorily.

If you do experience any difficulties your personal advisor [infill name of advisor] is always on hand to give you any technical support you need. The company's five-year warranty on all products means your [infill product] is covered for replacement parts and labour until [infill date] so you don't have to worry about any additional expense should any problems occur.

There are always new products coming onto the computer market and we would like to keep you up-to-date with those. In fact, you might be interested in [infill suitable product], which has recently become available. Remember [infill name of advisor] can help you with any questions you have and can advise you on the best and most competitively priced options available. Please feel free to call whenever you need to.

Thanks once again for your custom.

Yours sincerely,

Michael Brown

Michael Brown
Technical Support Manager

Figure 12-1: Personalising your mailshot.

Oyez is an office supply company that has come up with a clever way to personalise customer communication. Because it keeps details of customer purchases on a computer, it can generate a *Stockchecker* form for each customer, listing items they regularly buy and prompting them to either re-order or cross out what they don't need. This initiative benefits both Oyez (by encouraging repeat orders) and the customer (by helping them control their stock).

Being Creative with Personalised Mailshots

You don't have to draw a line after personalising names and addresses on letters. Look at the ideas shown in this list:

- **Make sure you use your customer's name and address.** And not just on your letter; you could, for example, put their name and address on the response device making it easier for them to complete.
- **Send birthday mailings.** If you know the birth dates of your customers, send them a special greeting. Rather than sending out mailings individually, you could send out birthday greetings for each month, and maybe include an offer that lasts until the end of the customer's 'birthday month'.
- **Prompt your customers with service reminder mailings.** If your products need regular servicing, create a reminder mailing. A letter is probably all you need for this mailshot.
- **Create a personalised order form.** Why not create a personalised order form for regular customers?

If you over-personalise your mailing, you risk appearing too familiar with your customers.

Chapter 13

Engaging Your Customers for Maximum Response

In This Chapter

- Offering your customers a carrot
- Making your customers feel involved in your mailshot

If you want to increase response to your direct mail offer, we offer two very effective ways in this chapter: Engage your customers by offering an incentive or create a sense of involvement by enclosing additional material.

TIP

Read through Chapter 6 for ideas on getting the best from your customers and turning them into an additional sales force.

Using Incentives in Your Mailings

The incentive you choose will depend on the business you're in and what you want to achieve. Table 13-1 gives you some ideas.

Table 13-1 Direct Mail Incentives

Type of incentive	*Best use*	*Ideas*
High volume	Generating lots of responses though not necessarily good sales leads	Free gifts, discount prices, sales, two-for-the-price-of-one offers, free prize draws, competitions

(continued)

Table 13-1 *(continued)*

Type of incentive	***Best use***	***Ideas***
Repeat purchase	Encouraging repeat purchases	Trade-in discounts, bulk order discounts, loyalty points, voucher offers
Speed	Aiming to get a quick response	Early bird incentives, limited time offers, limited edition offers
Confidence	Reducing the feeling of risk customers may have about a purchase	Money back guarantees, extended warranty offers, 'You can cancel your order at any time' offers, 'If you can find this cheaper any-where else' offers
Convenience	Aiming to offer the customer added convenience	Free delivery, interest-free credit

REMEMBER

Legal issues may affect some of these incentives. Chapter 14 contains more information on the legal aspects of direct mail.

Involving Your Customer in Your Mailing

Creating a sense of customer involvement with your mailshot can increase its effectiveness. Try these ideas:

- **Include a money-off or free voucher.**
- **Enclose a free sample.** But remember, restrictions apply to the size and type of sample you can send in an enve-lope. Contact Royal Mail to find out more.
- **Offer a free trial.**
- **Provide a free demonstration.** If this technique fails because customers are wary of the hard sell, why not reduce the pressure by creating an online demo or a

video demo or a demonstration evening that people are free to attend?

- **Enclose a relevant gimmick.** Here's an example: A time management consultancy enclosed stop-watches in its mailing and invited customers to time various tasks. The stop-watch was not only useful to the customer, it also provided a way for the company to demonstrate the importance of its service.

TRY THIS

Think inspiration!

If you're stuck for incentive-based inspiration, try these activities:

- Think about what types of incentives you could use to invite a speedy response to your mailing.
- Write a list of all the gimmicks you can think of that are relevant to your product.

Chapter 14

Keeping Your Mailshot Legal

In This Chapter

- Making sure your mailshot doesn't break the law
- Conducting prize draws and competitions legally

Don't spoil a good campaign by breaking the law.

This chapter aims to serve as a guide to the main legal issues surrounding mailings. Even so, it is not a substitute for professional advice, which should be sought if you have any doubts about the legality of your mailing.

Conducting Mailings Legally

Figure 14-1 shows a checklist designed to help you keep your mailshot legal.

In addition to the handy checklist shown in Figure 14-1, you must check you have permission to use the list to which you are mailing. Otherwise you risk breaking the law. For more information, visit the Direct Marketing Association's Web site on `www.dma.org.uk`.

Have you described your product or service in a true and fair manner?
Any mailshot which includes a false description of a product or service, whether about
its size, method of manufacture, history, performance and so on, constitutes an offence
under the Trade Descriptions Act 1968.
Have you been clear about the price of your product or service?
You cannot charge a higher price than the one advertised. Equally, you cannot advertise
a sales price if the product or service has not been advertised at a higher price for at
least 28 consecutive days in the previous 6 months.
Have you demanded payment for unsolicited goods?
If you send a product as part of your mailing which your prospect hasn't requested,
you cannot demand payment for this item. It is also your responsibility to collect the
item, not the customer's responsibility to send it back. Any items not collected after
six months become the property of the recipient.
Is any of the material in your mailing potentially offensive?
It is important to remember that your mailing may go to people with different cultural and
religious backgrounds. What may be acceptable to you, may not be acceptable to some
of your customers.

Figure 14-1: Keeping your mailshot within the law.

Abiding by the Data Protection Act

REMEMBER

You must comply with the requirements of the *Data Protection Act 1998*. In essence the Act says that people:

- Must be allowed to choose whether they want to disclose the information you request.
- Must also be told who is going to use the information (for example, if you are handing it on to a third party), why the information is wanted, and what use it will be put to.
- Must be allowed, based on the information in the previous bullet, to choose whether or not to receive any other mailings from you.

EXAMPLE

Include the following wording in your mailing:

> *From time to time we send out promotional material about our products. Please tick this box if you do not want to receive this material . . .*

Strict penalties are enforced for failing to comply with the Act. If you're in any doubt, contact the Data Protection Registrar (Tel: 01625 545 745).

Addressing monetary issues

The following issues must also be addressed if they affect your mailshot:

- **If selling financial products or services you must also comply with the Financial Services and Markets Act 2000.** For more information about this, contact The Financial Services Authority (Tel: 020 7066 1000).
- **If offering credit for the purchase of goods or services (payment schemes, for example), you must also comply with the Consumer Credit Act 1974.** Several issues surround disclosure of information, as well as governing form and content requirements. The Act also covers rates, conditions imposed, and mandatory cooling off periods. For more information contact The Office of Fair Trading (Tel: 020 7211 8000).

Handling Prize Draws and Competitions Legally

Two incentives in particular have strict laws governing their use:

- Prize draws
- Competitions

This section runs through the special considerations you need to know about.

What do I need to know about prize draws?

The most important thing to remember is that entry must be free and not conditional on any order or purchase. The selection of the winner must also be completely unbiased. It is illegal, for example, to select as the winner a regular customer who you want to reward.

What do I need to know about competitions?

Prizes in competitions are awarded on the basis of merit rather than simple luck. And while it is not illegal to charge an entry fee, if you do, you have to make sure there's a sufficient level of skill involved in winning, otherwise the competition could be deemed illegal.

Designing a competition legally

To stay on the right side of the law, a competition must have a skill element. The selection of the winner cannot be made randomly at any stage. So even if you have a quiz, you'll need to add a tie breaker so the judges can select the best entry from all the correct quiz entries. Don't use *forecasting* (such as the result of a football match), and always have at least one independent judge even if you have a panel. The rules of entry must be available prior to entry.

Rules of competition entry should include:

- A closing date
- Any intention to use the winners in publicity
- Any limit on the number of entries
- Any permissions required (for example, from a parent)
- Any requirement of proof of purchase
- Any restrictions on entrants (for example, 'You must be over 18')
- How and when the winners will be notified
- How and when the winners and results will be announced
- If a cash alternative can be substituted for any prize
- The judging criteria

- The nature of the prizes
- The promoter's full name and business address
- Where appropriate, who owns copyright on entries
- Whether and how entries will be returned by promoters

Chapter 15

Solving Common Creative Questions

In This Chapter

- Moving towards creative success
- Finding out what to include in your mailing
- Discovering the merits of long and short copy, photos, and illustrations

This chapter could have been titled 'All you ever wanted to know about creating mailshots, but were too afraid to ask'. But of course, that would have been too long to write in the running heads!

Here we present and answer the most common questions asked about the creative side of direct mail.

What Are the Most Important Factors for a Successful Mailing?

These are the three most important factors to remember:

- **List:** Target the right people
- **Offer:** Say the right thing . . .
- **Timing:** . . . at the right time

REMEMBER

Never lose sight of the fact that your mailshot is a one-to-one communication with your customer; make it personal, relevant, and interesting.

How Can I Make Sure I've Got Everything Right Creatively?

You're on track for success if your mailing does the following:

- Attracts the reader's attention
- Quickly establishes the relevance of your offer
- Convinces the reader of the benefits of your product
- Says what action you expect the reader to take
- Closes the sale (where relevant) with a powerful paragraph
- Takes the order (where relevant) by making it as easy as possible to respond

What's the Role of Each of the Creative Elements in My Mailing?

TIP

Think of your mailshot as a stand-in sales person. The envelope is the knock at the door, the letter is the product presentation, the brochure or leaflet is the demo, and the response device is the contract. So:

- Your envelope needs to create the right first impression
- Your letter headline needs a strong link with the envelope message
- Your opening paragraph should communicate your news immediately
- Your remaining paragraphs should tell the story in full
- Use facts and figures wherever possible

- Don't be vague about what you want your reader to do
- Make sure your letter has a strong closing paragraph
- Check that your leaflet or brochure brings your product to life
- Make sure your response device facilitates easy response

What Works Best, Long or Short Copy?

The key thing is making sure you tell the full story – how long this takes doesn't matter so much, provided your copy is relevant and interesting to read.

If your mailing has lots of copy, use the visual techniques described in Chapter 11 to help guide the reader through it.

Are Photographs Better Than Illustrations?

Photographs are generally more persuasive than illustrations. Their main strength is they show how a product actually looks. Cartoons can be effective too, provided they don't undermine the credibility of your product.

What Components Should I Definitely Include in My Mailing?

REMEMBER

No hard and fast rules govern this, though you need an envelope or carrier of some sort, a sales piece, and some sort of response device. What's known as a *one-piece mailing* combines all three – the envelope opens out into a letter and response device. Other mailshots choose to keep everything separate. Whatever you decide, each piece must actively sell or support your offer.

Part IV
Sorting Out Production and Dispatch

'In a previous life, before I became a lemming, I was a small company without a marketing plan.'

In this part . . .

This part deals with the technical processes involved in producing mailshots. It gives you a practical insight into how these processes work so that you're in a position to negotiate with professionals and set about some of the production tasks yourself. It also looks at sending out your mailshot, and coping with the responses you receive.

Chapter 16

Producing Your Mailshot

In This Chapter

- Achieving as much as you can without suppliers
- Producing letter mailings and leaflets
- Working with images
- Using a designer

This chapter introduces the themes involved in producing a mailshot. You have a choice of two ways forward – producing it yourself, or paying to get some professional help. You can read about both right here.

REMEMBER

Planning, planning, planning – even simple mailshots can go wrong if you don't plan carefully in advance. Set realistic deadlines and make sure you've talked to everyone involved. It pays to do a trial version of what you're after (a *dummy*) to make sure it works. Use codes to identify your mailing packs (they can be positioned discreetly within your response address or reply device), so you're able to track responses and save time with any customer queries.

Putting Together Your Own Mailing

All you really need to start producing your own mailshots is a computer and a printer – even a simple letter in an envelope can be effective provided you're targeting the right people with the right message.

Say you run an office stationery company and a competitor opens up around the corner. To ensure you don't lose custom, why not send a letter to your customers thanking them for using your service and offering them a small incentive to continue – perhaps 10 per cent off their next order.

In order to work out if such a basic mailshot is the answer for you, ask yourself the following:

- **Is my contact list already on my computer?** If not, then you might find it easier to put it onto a computer first, though if your mailshot is small, paper records will do.
- **Will a letter be enough to achieve my objectives?** This depends on the product or service you're offering and what you're trying to achieve.

If, after answering these questions you still feel a basic mailshot will suffice, then what are you waiting for? Get started by reading the next few sections.

Producing a Simple Letter Mailshot

All you need is a computer with a word processing program, a printer, paper, envelopes, and stamps!

Use a word processing program with a *mail merge* facility. This special feature saves you loads of time and effort by allowing you to type the letter just once and then leave the name, address, and other personal details blank. The computer does the rest by filling in these details automatically as the letters are printed. The mail merge facility also lets you start each letter with the recipient's name – a technique that's proven to increase responses.

Save yourself even more time and effort by using a word processing package that also prints labels. You can use mail merge to print them out as sheets so you don't have to address each envelope individually.

Producing a Mailshot with Pictures

Supposing you want to include a leaflet with your letter and, while you know what wording you want to use, you also want to incorporate pictures and make the whole thing look slick and professional.

What's the best approach? Decide how much you want to spend; your budget determines which of the following options you choose:

- **Hire a professional designer, marketing, or advertising agency.** This can be expensive but results in a high quality end product. Try to get a recommendation or research your options on the Internet.
- **Hire a professional freelance designer.** More cost-effective than the previous option, but unless you or someone you know and trust has already used the designer, this could be a bit of a gamble. So try to get a recommendation from a knowledgeable colleague.
- **Use a high street printer.** Many of these offer design services; your leaflet may not end up looking like a work of art but it won't cost as much either.
- **Do it yourself!** The alternative to paying someone else is to do it yourself on a computer with one of the many desktop publishing programs now available. These are affordable and have lots of features capable of producing high-quality mailshots.

TRY THIS: Put together a list of designers, and agencies from friends, the business press, the Internet, and any other sources you can think of. Can you narrow this list down to a chosen few?

Getting diagrams and pictures into a mailshot

Do the diagrams, charts, tables, maps, or whatever other artwork you plan to use already exist? Where are they stored?

- If they're on your computer, you should be able to simply copy and paste them.
- If they're on paper, they need to be scanned in first.

If they don't already exist, you'll need to brief a designer to generate them (see the section 'Getting What You Want from a Designer' for some helpful advice).

Using photographs in a mailshot

If you want to use a photograph that you don't already have, you'll need to source it. A designer might be able to source photography, keeping you abreast of costs. Otherwise, your choices are as follows:

- Hire a photographer to take the picture
- Take the picture yourself
- Hire or buy rights to a picture library image (known as *stock photography*)

Once the picture's taken, you can scan it in and alter it digitally – a process known as *retouching*. This can be very expensive, however, especially if you have to outsource to a designer or professional retoucher; it may prove more cost-effective to retake the picture. Thanks to the quality and sophistication of digital processing packages, the best option may well be to do it yourself.

REMEMBER

When commissioning photography or using images supplied by a photo library, you need to be absolutely clear about how you are going to use them and who owns the copyright.

Getting What You Want from a Designer

REMEMBER

The quality of your finished product depends on how well you brief the designer. Communicating what you want and, just as importantly, what you don't want, is the key.

Make sure you communicate the following:

- Exactly what you need to include (how much text, how many pictures, if you have a response device, and so on, as well as the degree of prominence each should have)
- Any size restrictions
- The number of pages
- Whether you want colour or black and white (this has important cost implications)

Either give your designer a budget to work to, or tell her what you want and get her to supply a quote (get a couple of quotes from different designers to assess your best option).

Generally speaking, the more you want, the more you'll have to pay – not necessarily at the design stage, but certainly at the printing and mailing stages.

Chapter 17

Making Use of a Printing Company

In This Chapter

- Sourcing a supplier for simple print work
- Considering the cost of professional printing
- Supplying print-ready material in the right way

If you decide that your mailshot will benefit from the added impact of professionally printed content, this chapter is for you. It guides you through finding a suitable printing company, letting them know what you want, working out what it will cost you, and providing your printer with materials in the best possible way.

Finding and Working With a Printer

Draw up a list of local printers – ask friends and business contacts for recommendations, and look in the business press and directories, or on the Internet. If you have time, visit the printers for a quote rather than getting one over the phone (this gives you an idea of how they work, and how helpful and efficient they are).

Before quoting for the work, a printer needs to know:

- How you'll supply text.
- How many names and addresses are on your list.

- What weight and size of paper and envelopes you want.
- What type of paper (known as *stock*) you want to use.
- If you want addresses printed directly onto envelopes or onto labels.
- What typefaces you want to use.
- If you want the printer to enclose the letter or if you're, for example, using a mailing house. (Someone has to actually stick on stamps and post your mailings.)
- How you want the job delivered.
- When you need the mailshot finished by.

REMEMBER

Prices quoted by printers may not include VAT.

After obtaining quotes and deciding on which printer to use, expect to work to a schedule like this one:

1. **Obtain an *estimate* (your quote) and agree a price before work begins.**
2. **Agree a schedule for the work well in advance.**
3. **Ensure copy is supplied on disk with *hard copy* (that is, a printed or paper version) attached.**
4. **Supply any colour visuals on a disk or CD.**
5. **Check and proof artwork rigorously.** Print houses usually have in-house proofreaders to check for mistakes, but you are ultimately responsible. Any errors you notice after the artwork has been signed off are usually very expensive to correct.

When you've got your quote and opted for your preferred printer, you enter the *artwork stage*. Artwork is what you supply to your printer to print from, and encompasses everything you're supplying to the printer (curiously enough, it's not just the artwork but the text too!). This is almost always supplied digitally.

TIP

You or your designer should prepare a hard copy document for your printer's reference. Inside the document, make sure that all the text is in the right place, all the fonts and colours are as you've chosen, and all images and diagrams are correctly positioned. This cuts down the chances of your printer making an error with your work.

Some issues to consider at this stage include:

- **Whether you're supplying data that's Mac or PC generated.** Your printer might need to know this.
- **What format disk to supply files on.** The printer might need to know whether this is DVD, CD, Zip disk, or a normal floppy disk.
- **Whether or not you require a proof.** A *proof* is a test version of the pages, showing what they will look like when properly printed. You'll also need to consider whether you want a laser-printed proof or a PDF (electronic) one.
- **What your deadlines and quoted prices are.** You should already know these, as should your printer, but there's no harm double-checking!

Working Out How Much a Printer Costs

Printers usually have fixed price bands. Figure 17-1 shows some examples, though prices differ depending on individual printers and exactly what you supply them with.

REMEMBER

When deciding the amount of material you want printed, remember that the *economies of scale* rule applies: The more you print the cheaper per unit it'll work out.

Quantity	1–500	501–1,000	1,001–5,000
Single-sided one-page black & white A5 leaflet with no photographs or diagrams	£35	£45	£110
Double-sided, one-colour A5 leaflet with 3 photographs	£120	£150	£180
One-colour, one-third A4 leaflet, folded, with photographs	£120	£150	£250
4-page black & white A4 leaflet with diagrams but no photographs	£150	£190	£550
4-page A4 colour leaflet with 5 photographs and 1 black & white diagram	£750	£1,000	£1,500

Figure 17-1: Sample print prices.

Printing processes use a different rendering of colour to that seen on a computer screen; computers use red, green, and blue (known as *RGB*), while printers use cyan, magenta, yellow, and black (known as *CMYK* – 'K' for black) to generate the printing plates. Try to supply colour material generated using the CMYK process. You could always ask for a proof to check for variations in colour, but remember there's a charge for this.

If using a professional graphics software program like Adobe PageMaker or QuarkXPress, the conversions your files undergo to be compatible with printing processes can be achieved within your software. But if you're using applications such as Microsoft Office, your printing company will need to do the necessary conversions, for which there is an additional charge.

Supplying Images to a Printer Correctly

Supplying text to a printer is usually very straightforward – most printers can accept any word processing or typesetting file and print from that. Artwork can be a little trickier.

If in any doubt about how images should be supplied, talk to both your designer and printer to come to a suitable arrangement. Better still, get them to talk to each other.

Digital imagery has come a long way in recent years, and provided you have sufficient *dpi* (dots per inch, relating to the clarity of your image) in your image, the results can look extremely crisp. The bigger you blow up your image relative to its original size, the more you lose *resolution* (meaning the image becomes more blurry).

Images may sometimes be supplied as transparencies; if this is the case, they need to be scanned in before they can be reproduced in your mailshot.

Always make sure you're not infringing copyright restrictions if you use an image that has appeared elsewhere.

Chapter 18

Using a Mailing Database to Aid Production

In This Chapter

- Maintaining your database to assist mailshot production
- Supplying your mailing list to printers

Data processing (also sometimes called *address management*) is the inputting and management of the names and addresses of the people you're sending your mailing to – in short, managing your mailing list pre-posting. A well-managed mailing list really helps you (or your printer, if you're using one) out when you're producing your mailshot. Your entire campaign can be undermined if you don't pay careful attention to this aspect of direct mail; in a recent sample of mailshot recipients, 85 per cent agreed that inaccuracies of name and address reflected badly on the company.

Accuracy of information is key. An up-to-date database:

- Increases response rates.
- Reduces production and postage costs, for example, by eliminating duplications.
- Helps ensure compliance with data protection regulations.

Ensuring Your Database Is in Good Order

Five basic data processing principles ensure a high degree of accuracy:

- **Your database's use dictates your address management systems, not vice versa.** For example, if you mail your customers on the basis of their purchases, make sure your database can select relevant dates and products.
- **Everyone with access to your database uses a common system for obtaining and inputting names and addresses.**
- **Check newly acquired information.** If you put poor quality information in, you'll get poor quality information out. Always check information against the most up-to-date reference data – for instance, the Royal Mail postal code checker, which is available online.
- **Check for gone aways and duplicates on a regular basis.** *Gone aways* are people who no longer live at the address you hold for them. Print a return address on all of your mailings to help you keep track of this.
- **Check your list against that of the Mailing Preference Service (`www.mpsonline.org.uk`).** This is a list of people who have exercised their right not to receive unsolicited mail, and using it is a legal obligation.

Supplying Your Mailing List to Your Printer

Check with your printer to see what mailing list delivery format they require – for example, on a disk or e-mailed? Make sure your data is laid out in such a way that your printer can make use of it. Standard practice is to supply a file layout with your list showing what is on each record and what data is to be used in the letter.

Improving your own database

Try these exercises out to aid database management:

- Using a random sample from your database, check to see what percentage are still correct.
- Work out how you would go about updating your database.
- Draw up a code of practice for your data capture.

Figure 18-1 shows an example of file layout as supplied to a printer.

Example File layout

FIELD	
Contact Name:	Adam Sample
Job Title:	Manager
Company Name:	Samples Ltd
Address Line 1:	1 Sample Street
Address Line 2:	SAMPLE TOWN
Postcode:	SSS 123
Campaign Code:	1234
Contact Serial No:	2808
Job Code:	37
Segment Code:	3
Salutation:	Dear

Figure 18-1: An example file layout as supplied to a mailshot printer.

Chapter 19

Handling Responses to Your Mailing

In This Chapter

- Getting ready to receive responses
- Organising your dispatch procedure
- Avoiding being swamped by responses

If you've not sorted out your response method by the time you're getting your mailshot printed, now's the time to do it!

If you haven't planned how to deal with your responses well in advance of your mailing, warm prospects can quickly turn to cold shoulders. Being prepared can mean anything from having sufficient staff to send out requested information promptly to having enough of the mail-order product you're promoting in stock.

Working Out What Happens after a Mailing Goes Out

If you've done everything right, orders and enquiries should start coming in within 3–7 days. When this happens, they need to be proccssed or sorted into groups: Single orders, multiple orders, and general enquiries, for example.

TIP: Code your different groups for ease of checking and sorting.

Any payments need to be verified and recorded, and then, finally, the order can be *fulfilled,* which means supplying your product or service to the customer. Figure 19-1 shows a suitable system for handling responses.

Draw a flow-chart or diagram like that shown in Figure 19-1 of your current response handling and order fulfillment procedures. Is there any room for improvement?

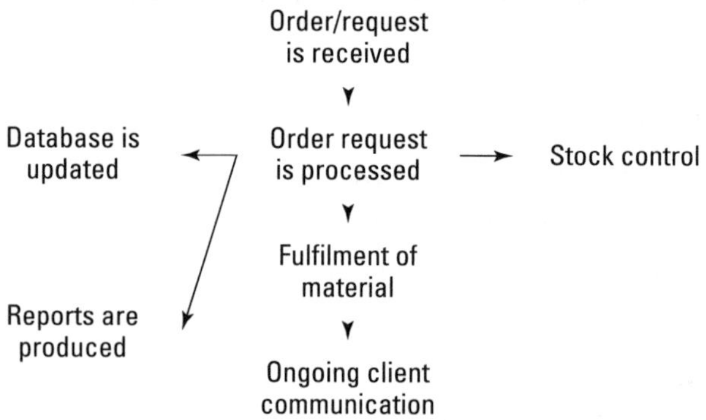

Figure 19-1: A workable method of handling responses.

Recording helpful data for the present and the future

Data capture is all about thinking ahead. Recording each customer and order details could seem like a hassle now, but could save you a lot of trouble in the future. Every response you get tells you something about your customer, so think of it as an opportunity to refine your customer database.

Handling stock control

Be aware of how much stock is going in and out, so that you can adequately supply customers responding to your offer as well as any other random orders.

Non-supply of goods has legal and regulatory implications, so be sure to consider exactly how much stock you need.

Sorting Out Dispatch Arrangements

The way you deal with your customer's response – be it by e-mail, reply device, fax, phone, or in person – is *response handling*. *Fulfilment* is when you supply the customer with something as a result of their response.

The moment of truth comes when you move from response to fulfilment – don't slip up now! Before dispatching orders check them carefully and record all relevant data. In fact, don't just check, double check to make sure you've got the right item, quantity, colour, size, and so on. Make sure everything's securely packed and properly addressed, and do it all quickly!

TIP: In case anything goes wrong, make sure you have some sort of Customer Service facility in place to deal with any complaints – and that's where the data you've recorded during dispatch comes in handy.

Avoiding Common Pitfalls

The answer to successful dispatch, quite simply, is to plan every aspect of your campaign, right from the beginning. Figure 19-2 shows a checklist to help you out.

Staying out of the response swamp

Don't get swamped by your responses! A simple way of avoiding this is to stagger your mailshots. Provided it's not time-critical (for example, seasonal direct mail), send your mailshot out in batches, leaving enough time between to make sure you can deal with responses and fulfilment. You may lose out on certain postal discounts by not sending everything at once, but if the alternative is disappointing your customers, this approach is worthwhile.

Timings – do you have schedules for all key dates of the campaign, including cut-off dates and a plan to deal with requests that come in after the cut-off dates?
How are responses to be received – via mail, e-mail, telephone, fax?
What are the postal/phone requirements? Should a reply-paid response address/freephone/fax number or e-mail address be set up?
Have you estimated how many responses you will receive?
Turn-around of response for optimum timing
Mailing dates – have they been set and how likely are they to change?
Source coding – have you decided which codes you will need and how they will appear in your mailing?
Coupon/response device – what information does it hold and what needs to be data captured?
Is the coupon/response device easily handled/legible/big enough?
Is the response/mailing code clear, easy to read and unique to the source?
Returns – how will these be processed?
Methods of payment and monies involved – cash/cheque/postal orders/credit cards/ charge cards/standing order/direct debit, etc.
What other information is required for the data capture?
What information is to be held on the database and how is it to be used?
What are the contingency plans for unexpectedly high response levels?
What reporting is required?
What materials need to be supplied to the responder – when and by who? How long have you allowed from receipt of response to material going out – for stock replenishment etc?
Have you covered all legal issues and data protection?
Staffing – have you considered both staffing levels and how you are going to keep everybody informed of what is going on?

Figure 19-2: Checklist for avoiding dispatch problems.

Using the info you get back

A mailshot is a great opportunity to update and refine your database, which can help you target more accurately in the future (see Chapter 4 for more on gathering customer data). You can:

- Check names and addresses are up-to-date
- Include a few simple questions in your reply device to garner a little more customer information

To be most effective, whoever handles the response to your mailing needs to have access to or a copy of your database.

REMEMBER

Response information is covered by the Data Protection Act (see Chapter 14 for more details).

TIP

If you've coded your different mailshots, use these to find out which versions of your mailshot worked best with which customer.

Part V

The Part of Tens

'You're not quite what I expected.'

In this part . . .

Every *For Dummies* book contains a Part of Tens. Sit down with this part to glean some more facts and ideas for your direct mail campaign. We include a list of tests to try out on your mailshot to make it even better, and some more general direct mail facts you may be interested to read.

Chapter 20

Ten Great Ideas to Improve Mailshot Effectiveness

Here are ten great ways to test your direct mail's effectiveness – today.

Try out these simple ways to improve your mailshots:

- **Change the headline on your letter.** Your letter headline is the hook on which your message relies. So whilst the benefits your product has may not change, your opening line can.
- **Change the timing of your mailshot.** Try varying the day of the week, time of month, and even the month itself (but not if you have a seasonal product or service, of course!).
- **Focus on a different product benefit.** If you're lucky enough to have several product benefits, vary the benefit you focus on to see which gets the best response.
- **Get the right message to the right people.** Send different messages to different customers – young or old, married or single, rural or urban, regular or occasional users.
- **Include a brochure as well as a letter.** Often a letter is enough, but at times, you can't get all the detail you need into a letter. If you sell complex products or have a wide range of products, try adding a brochure. Brochures also work well if you are selling a product that has a long sales consideration time.
- **Include a free gift.** The appeal of free gifts does depend on what product and service you are promoting. If your message is relevant, a gift can tip people over to respond.

- **Learn from experience.** Use your direct mail not just to improve your customer data but also to develop your planning and design skills. Become involved in the whole process . . . and be even better next time!
- **Offer a payment option such as interest free credit.** Look at this if you sell high value goods or services – it may be the difference between a response and not (being one less thing for the potential buyer to worry about).
- **Provide an early-bird incentive.** See if you can prompt early action and early response by limiting the time that an offer or incentive is in place for.
- **Test freephone number against an ordinary telephone number.** It's unlikely that a standard telephone number will stop people who really want to respond from doing so, but you may put off people by not offering a free-phone number. Offering a freephone number also says a lot about how your business treats its customers.

Chapter 21

Ten Things You Didn't Know About Direct Mail

We call this chapter the *Anorak Chapter* – it won't help you produce your mailshot, but does give you some pretty impressive stats to chew over when you're considering your next mailshot.

You don't need to read this section of the book, but next time you're stuck for a conversation down at the pub, why not startle your friends with these facts? Or perhaps not! Read on:

- 5,438 million items were mailed in 2003 (up 3.9 per cent from 2002), with 22 per cent being business mailings.
- The overall volume of direct mail has increased by 139 per cent in the last 13 years.
- £2,467 million was spent on direct mail advertising in 2003.
- Money spent on direct mail has increased by 165 per cent in the last 13 years.
- It's estimated that consumer direct mail generates nearly £27 million worth of business every year.
- For every 31p spent, £14 is generated.
- The average British household receives 14.1 items of direct mail every four weeks.
- 60 per cent of consumer direct mail is opened, 40 per cent is opened and read, and 13 per cent is kept to read later or passed on to someone else.
- 37 per cent of consumers have responded to direct mail at least once in the 12 months between 2002–2003.
- Geographically, those in the north of Britain spend more through direct mail than those in the south.